T4-APS-533

Chapel Talks

Other books by C. B. Eavey:

Principles of Teaching for Christian Teachers

Principles of Personality Building for Christian Parents

Principles of Mental Health for Christian Living

Principles of Christian Ethics

Practical Christian Ethics

The Art of Effective Teaching

How To Be an Effective Sunday School Teacher

Ninety-five Brief Talks for Various Occasions

Talks to Young People

2500 Sentence Sermons

Each Day

Starting Branch Sunday Schools

Chapel Talks

by C. B. Eavey

BAKER BOOK HOUSE
Grand Rapids 6, Michigan
1959

Printed in United States of America

Contents

Preface

A thoughtful mind, when it receives truths from without, goes to work upon them, combining them with the results of past experience and learning. The outcome is a completed product that may be a source of profit and blessing both to him who thinks and to those who may hear a message delivered by the thinker.

The purpose of this book is to provide truths as a basis for such thinking and speaking. It is hoped that what is presented in the book will be found valuable for use by chapel speakers, ministers, and young people's workers—anyone who may from time to time give addresses and sermons to the young.

The author of the book also entertains the hope that young people who read it for themselves may be stimulated, edified, inspired, and challenged by the messages therein contained. In the measure that young people obtain something, either indirectly or directly, that results in their being brought more fully into the purpose of God for their lives, the work of the author in preparing the book will not have been in vain.

C. B. Eavey.

1

Appetite

"The kingdom of God is not meat and drink"
(Romans 14:17).

Did you ever have to eat when you did not want food? If you did, you know it is not easy to satisfy a need apart from desire, that is, without appetite. You have many needs besides the need for food, therefore, you have many hungers, many cravings, many longings. That is, you have many appetites or, perhaps it is more correct to say, appetite for many things. And you may be harmed less from not being able to indulge appetite than from over-indulgence of appetite.

Young people of today live in a world that makes many appeals to the appetites. As a consequence, they are in danger of over-indulgence and thus of damage to health and well-being of body, mind, and soul. We are so made that the greater the abundance around us, the more we are inclined to indulge our appetite. Easy indulgence naturally leads to over-indulgence. The more we have to satisfy our needs, the more wants we have. When we live in the midst of plenty, we face the peril of developing abnormal or perverted appetites. The satisfying of unnatural appetites upsets the balance of our organism and causes a diseased condition.

In respect to the indulgence of appetite and the management of your life, you cannot follow the standards of men at large, except at your peril. If you would live on the highest level, you must have your own standards. In general, the corrupt part of human nature rules over the spiritual. Appetite takes first place and enslaves the noble faculties of mind and heart.

"Put a knife to thy throat, if thou be a man given to appetite," is the advice of Solomon (Proverbs 23:2). Indulgence of appetite to gratify the senses is a sin that easily besets us. When plenty abounds, we need be much on our guard. We must realize that we are in danger and we must choose carefully that which is best for us. "Reason should direct, and appetite obey," says Cicero. We must restrain our craving appetite as if our throat were cut rather than indulge ourselves in merely giving pleasure to the senses.

Appetite is God-given. It is something to be used, not abused and perverted. Proper and normal gratification makes for physical, mental, moral, and spiritual well-being. Perversion of appetite by excesses pleasing only to the flesh destroys health and makes impossible the lawful and normal enjoyment of those things which God provides for our use and well being. To live on the highest level, you must "be temperate in all things." Temperance prevents indulgence to excess which, feeding upon itself, makes it constantly more and more difficult to satisfy the appetite.

Pleasing the senses through over-indulging the appetite harms the soul. It unfits the heart for the service of God, it alienates the mind from spiritual joys, and it spoils the relish for what is pleasing to God. Constantly you must examine yourself. If you find yourself prone to pleasing only the flesh, you must do these two things: take up arms against temptation from without to yield to appetite; subdue the tendencies within which prompt carnal desire. To live as God would have you live, you must choose rather to punish your appetite than to be punished by it.

He who tastes and sees "that the Lord is good" is so blessed in trusting Him as to find that "he satisfieth the longing soul, and filleth the hungry soul with goodness" (Psalms 107:9).

2

Assurance

"Let us draw near with a true heart in full assurance of faith" (Hebrews 10:22).

Are you a Christian? Does Christ live in you? Are you sure that you are right with God? Many Christians, especially young ones, are troubled by such questions. Sometimes when they are feeling good and are able to conquer their sins, they think that all is well with their soul. At other times they are very sure all is not well. You need not be uncertain. You are either saved or lost, and you can know for sure which is true.

You will make no progress in your spiritual life until you are certain. So long as you do not know that the foundation is securely laid, you will be wavering between faith and doubt. One time you will be up and another time you will be down, and you will get nowhere. How can you be sure? The answer is, through a study of God's Word. Jesus said, "Search the Scriptures; for in them ye think ye have eternal life: and they are they which testify of me" (John 5:39).

The foundation of the Christian life is Jesus Christ, the Son of God and the Saviour of men. In His death on the cross He effected your salvation. Nothing you can do will give you right standing before God. First, last, and always, it is the blood of Christ that makes atonement for your lost soul. You contribute not an iota to your salvation. With Wesley you have to say, "Other refuge have I none, hangs my helpless soul on Thee." Your feeling right or wrong has nothing whatever to do with your salvation. What you do, or do not do, is without merit in the sight of God. We are saved because Christ died for our sins. When Satan tortures you with doubts, meet his attacks with the fact that Christ died for you. If you feel yourself sinful, vile, and wholly unworthy, remind yourself that it was for such that He died. The basic support for your certainty is the complete and absolute efficacy of Christ's death.

To be certain, you need also to realize that your faith is completely effective. The blood of Christ procures your salvation but you must respond by receiving (John 1:12). There must be a response on your part, and your part is to "believe on his name." "He that believeth on him is not condemned" (John 3:18). Only faith, nothing you do, say, suffer, or give up, makes Christ's death efficacious in your case. But faith is absolutely sufficient. "He that heareth my word, and believeth on him that sent me, hath everlasting life, and shall not come into condemnation; but is passed from death unto life" (John 5:24). Are you troubled as to your faith? Do you doubt if you have believed? G. Campbell Morgan said that he always met such oft-repeated attacks of Satan by saying, "Lord, if I have never believed before, I now believe that Christ died for me."

Finally, you must be convinced of the complete and absolute reliability of the Word of God. What God says He means and He means what He says. He keeps His promises, and His Word is filled with promises to the believer. He has said that those who trust in Him shall be as "mount Zion, which cannot be removed, but abideth for ever" (Psalms 125:1). He has said, "I will never leave thee, nor forsake thee" (Hebrews 13:5). Make His promises personal to yourself; they are as much for you as they are for any other believer.

However you may feel, the facts remain: Christ died for you; by faith you have received Him. What God has said will stand after heaven and earth have passed away. You need not be concerned as to whether you feel right. That upon which you must concentrate is the facts. Resting upon these will not do away with temptation, sins, problems, difficulties, and failures but it will give you a permanent foundation.

3

Attractiveness

"Draw me, we will run after thee"
(Song of Solomon 1:4).

She was a young woman who, as the saying goes, "had not been around when good looks were given out." But, nevertheless, she was an attractive young woman. People were drawn to her and liked her. Seldom did anyone who knew her think about her lack of beauty. She had done well in making the most of what nature gave her. She lived a happy, wholesome life, so filled with healthful interests, that she had no time to spend in morbid thinking about herself. Her interest in others was genuine, drawing them to her. Whether or not she was familiar with George Washington's maxim to the effect that every action in company ought to be performed with others in mind, she observed it, making everyone feel at ease.

What can you do to make yourself attractive to other people? The old saying that "handsome is as handsome does" expresses a truth that you ought never to forget. Yet, it is important that you take care of matters having to do with your bodily appearance. You cannot change the color of your skin or the shape of your face. But some of your physical characteristics can be changed or modified. Whatever "looks" you received when you were born, you can do something to improve upon them. Using to good advantage what you have instead of moaning over what you do not have, is an element in attractiveness.

To be attractive pay attention to cleanliness which, Benjamin Franklin said, is "next to godliness." If you have so little respect for yourself that you do not keep yourself clean and tidy, you cannot reasonably expect other people to be drawn to you. To keep yourself so will take some time, but it pays big dividends.

Frequent bathing, regular brushing of the teeth, daily scrubbing of the hands, keeping the fingernails trimmed and clean, brushing the hair and washing it frequently, and keeping it combed, are things that add to your attractiveness. Clothes do not make the man. But they help a lot if they are clean and neat, even if they are not the finest.

If you are a girl, you have the problem of make-up. This is a sound rule: a little is better than too much. Do not spoil your natural attractiveness; use sparingly the kind of cosmetics that emphasize your best features. If you are a boy, your problem is shaving. Even if there is little to remove, a daily shave may be advisable. Girl or boy, you must consider haircuts. Have the haircut or hair style that best fits the shape of your face, your height, and your build. Choose the one that looks best for you.

Give attention to posture. Maybe you think you are too tall or too short. Whatever your height, you will feel better and look better if you do not stoop or slouch. Develop an erect, well-balanced posture and walk, then people will not notice so much your tallness or your shortness.

Are you too fat or too thin? Diet is the remedy for either condition. With intelligent care you can choose the foods that will add to your attractiveness and at the same time do much for your energy and health. Good eating habits are the means not only for control of weight but also for good health which makes for enjoyment of life and contribution to the lives of others.

Cultivate wholesome emotions, for emotions affect your appearance, your health, and your bearing. Tenseness, irritability, and fear hinder you in your relations with others. Your attitudes toward life have much effect on the appeal you make to others. The manner in which you meet problems and difficulties commends you to your fellows or turns them away from you. Worry and anxiety are deadly enemies to health and well-being and detract from your attractiveness.

4

The Bible

"I have more understanding than all my teachers: for thy testimonies are my meditation"
(Psalm 119:99).

Dr. Clarence E. Macartney, on a Sunday morning two days before he died, said to his brother who was leaving to preach in a nearby church, "Put all the Bible you can into your preaching." Information about the issues of the day, understanding of national and international problems, discussions of race relations, and enlightenment concerning moral matters, do not suffice. What men need is the Bible.

The Bible contains "the mind of God, the state of man, the way of salvation, the doom of sinners, and the happiness of believers. Its doctrines are holy, its precepts are binding, its histories are true, and its decisions are immutable." If you would be wise, you must read the Bible; if you would be safe, you must believe its message; if you would be holy, you must practice its teachings. It has light to direct you, food to nourish you, and comfort to cheer you. "It is the traveller's map, the pilgrim's staff, the pilot's compass, the soldier's sword, and the Christian's charter."

William Lyons Phelps said, "I thoroughly believe in a university education for men and women, but I believe a knowledge of the Bible without a college course is more valuable than a college course without the Bible." Tennyson said reading and knowing the Bible constitutes "an education in itself." Any person who deprives himself of a knowledge of the Bible "has deprived himself of the best there is in the world," said Woodrow Wilson.

No amount of education will do you any good if you do not

know the will of God for your life. All the learning you can gain is nothing if you are ignorant of your state in the sight of God and of the way of salvation He has provided in Christ. You are more than mind to be filled with knowledge; you are a living spirit created by God, not to be doomed to everlasting punishment in hell but to eternal happiness in heaven with Him. You are not a being who sojourns a few short years in this world but an everlasting spirit who lives on and on through the ceaseless ages of a never-ending eternity.

The Bible is the Book which gives you education for the life that is yours now and forevermore if you are God's child. Other books are for man, the creature; the Bible is for man, the spirit made in the image of God. The content of other books gives us information we need for an earthly existence; the Bible gives us knowledge we must have as heavenly spirits destined for a heavenly existence.

Read the Bible slowly, read it carefully, read it frequently, read it prayerfully. Study it intensively. Preachers and teachers may help you much in gaining knowledge of its precious truths, but what you learn yourself from searching its sacred pages will mean far more to you for time and for eternity than anything you gain from men. One truth you make your own from the Bible itself is worth a thousand you glean from books written or sermons delivered by other men.

5

Books and Reading

"The cloak that I left at Troas with Carpus, when thou comest, bring with thee, and the books"
(II Timothy 4:13).

Paul was a prisoner. He bids Timothy to come to him and as he comes through Troas, to bring with him the things he had left there, a cloak and books. Paul wanted the company of Timothy, protection for his body, and food for thought. Alone in prison, he felt the need of fellowship with a kindred spirit. In a cold cell, he stood in need of a warm cloak to help keep his body warm. In the loneliness of his hours as a prisoner, he could find solace in reading books. He who was guided by divine inspiration in the writing of a goodly portion of the New Testament would yet have his books with him. He had exhorted Timothy to give attention to reading. This he did himself, though he was now ready to depart to be with Christ. As long as he lived, he would continue to profit from the reading of books.

Today there are books and books and more books. We have books that are good, books that are indifferent, and books that are bad. We have books on almost every phase of every imaginable subject. We have books for entertainment, to pass the time, pleasant fiction and stories, books for general knowledge, books on technical subjects, books that deal with precious truth and excellent wisdom, books that treat sacred things. We can amuse ourselves with books, inform and instruct ourselves with books, inspire and elevate ourselves with books.

Without a love for good books, the richest person is poor. Someone once remarked that "a book is the lifeblood of its author." There is truth in the statement, for the cost to the author of a worthwhile book is not insignificant. A tremendous amount of thought and energy goes into the writing of any good book. The message of such a book enriches the thought and the life of the careful reader. Nobody knows just what a book is and nobody knows how or why it carries influence to mind and soul. These are mysteries for which there is no explanation. Nevertheless, the fact remains that a book creates for the reader an atmosphere that is potent in its effect on him. Rich indeed is he who loves books from the pages of which words leap out, delivering something invisible to the eyes that is translated into elements of enriched mental life or noble and elevated character.

A test of the worth of a book is the number of times you can read it with profit. A book that can be dipped into lightly gives forth a light message. There are so many good books that it is worse than a waste of time to read even one that does not make you a better person in mind, personality, and character. It is a poor book indeed that does not bear at least a second reading. The better the book, the greater the number of times you can read it with benefit to yourself. The best books do not yield to the reader all the riches of their content except as they are read again and again. Every reading of a really worthwhile book brings to mind and thought and heart of the reader something he did not get from any previous reading.

You should be as careful of the books you read as of the company you keep, because your character will be influenced as much by the one as the other. Just as the influence of a person creeps subtly into your own life, so the mysterious influence of a book steals into your being, making you either richer or poorer in respect to things of real worth. So positive is the effect of books and reading on life and character that it can be said, Tell me what you read and I will tell you what you are.

6

The Wonderful Christ

"His name shall be called Wonderful" (Isaiah 9:6).

"Wonderful" is a word used often in connection with divine activity. Christ is justly called "wonderful," for He is both God and man. Wonderful promises told of His coming into the world. He was wonderful in His birth, His life, His death, His resurrection, and His ascension. A constant series of wonders attended His entire earthly career. Without question, wonderful was the mystery of godliness concerning Him. Since He ascended into heaven, He has been doing wonders among men on earth. The greatest of all wonders is His bringing a soul from death unto eternal life.

He lived a wonderful life. It was a life of faith, it was a life filled with God, it was the life of God lived out in a man on earth who had the experiences common to men but who lived as never man lived. Those who met Him but once, those who saw Him frequently, those who knew Him intimately from constant association—all marvelled at what they saw in Him. The wonder grew that any man could do what He did.

He rendered a wonderful service. He pleased not Himself—an achievement no other man ever realized. He did not consider His own ease, safety, or pleasure; He did not seek His own will; He did not consult His own honor. He emptied Himself, making Himself of no reputation for the sake of men, to bring in a righteousness for us. His whole life was a self-denying life, foreign to human ways of thinking and living.

He was wonderful in victory. Opposed by the forces of hell, He came out conqueror over all, including death and the grave. The devil himself tempted Him unsuccessfully. Men of various classes were arrayed against Him—men of ability, men of keen insight, men of great power—but never once did they succeed in their many efforts to entangle Him. Even His enemies had to say, "Never man spake like this man." Enraged by their inability to overthrow Him, His enemies finally brought Him by false accusation down to the grave through the death on the cross. But He arose, triumphant over the grave itself.

He was wonderful in His death. The Roman officer who had charge of His execution was so impressed that he was moved to say that He was surely the Son of God. So marvelous was His death that Napoleon exclaimed, "If Socrates died like a man, then Jesus Christ died like a god."

From the grave He arose in a wonderful resurrection. His closest followers thought His death ended all and went their way. Soldiers on guard at His tomb became as dead men in the matchless light of His glorious coming forth from the grave. He had told His disciples many times prior to His crucifixion and death that He would arise from the dead, yet they had difficulty in believing it, even after they had seen Him and talked with Him.

He lives today in wonderful power—power to save to the uttermost any and all who come to God through Him, to give help to any that are tempted, to strengthen with might those who trust in Him, to make them more than conquerors, to supply all their needs, to do what is apparently impossible, and finally to make them stand in His glorious presence faultless and full of everlasting joy. Is it to be wondered at that the name of such a One should be called "Wonderful"?

7

Crucifixion

"God forbid that I should glory, save in the cross of our Lord Jesus Christ, by whom the world is crucified unto me, and I unto the world"
(Galatians 6:14).

To glory in a thing means to find satisfaction in that thing and to boast about it. We are so constituted that we are obliged to glory in something. The natural tendency is to try to find our satisfaction in the things of this world.

In Jeremiah 9:23 God tells us of three things we should not glory in. The first of these is wisdom. This, in the estimation of men in general, is the best of the three. Through the ages a high valuation has been placed on wisdom. However, the wisdom of man is foolishness with God. God pronounces woe upon them that are wise in their own eyes (Isaiah 5:21). Paul tells us in the first chapter of Romans that men became fools though they professed strong confidence in their wisdom. All the wisdom of man is going to perish. So we have no reason to glory in our wisdom.

The second thing God tells us not to glory in is might or strength. Samson gloried in his physical strength and came to a sad end. Tennyson says, "My strength is as the strength of ten because my heart is pure." But the heart of man is most deceitful and desperately wicked. Just when we think we are strong morally, we may have a fall which shows utter and unexpected weakness. A number of men whose names appear in the Bible record failed at the point in which they were strongest, e.g., Moses, Abraham, David. There are people who find much satisfaction in and do notable things because of the strength of their personality. But the Word of God tells us that things are done, not by might nor by power but by the Spirit of God. So we have no reason to glory in our might, be it might of body, or moral integrity, or of personality.

The third thing we are not to glory in is riches. A Midas is poor when he has nothing but gold; he cannot eat it or be loved by it. God said "Thou fool" to the man whose wealth so increased that he had to pull down his places of storage and build larger ones. If riches increase, we are not to set our heart upon them. Jesus told us not to lay up earthly treasure which we have today and do not have tomorrow. We have no reason to glory in our riches.

There is nothing in this world that we can glory in, nothing that brings unalloyed satisfaction, nothing that we can depend upon. All that is in the world is going to pass away soon—perhaps much sooner than we know. But we can glory in what our Lord accomplished for us on the cross. When He died there, the power of the world to rule over us was destroyed and we, dying in Christ, became dead to the world—a double death. Moreover, when Christ died, we entered into life. "I am crucified with Christ: nevertheless I live; yet not I, but Christ liveth in me: and the life which I now live in the flesh I live by the faith of the Son of God, who loved me, and gave himself for me" (Galatians 2:20).

The result is true glorying, or finding true satisfaction; for God is the only source of real satisfaction. Not wisdom, might, riches, or anything this world can offer gives us abiding satisfaction; only God can do that. "Let him that glorieth glory in this, that he understandeth and knoweth me, that I am the Lord" (Jeremiah 9:24). Thanks be unto our God for a Saviour who makes it possible for us to know God to the complete satisfying of every longing of the soul.

8

Difficulties in Doing Right

"Let your conversation be as it becometh the gospel of Christ" (Philippians 1:27).

This verse might be rendered thus: "Lead lives worthy of the gospel" or "Practice living so as to show forth the truth of the gospel." The thought is that those who are Christians should do the things that are right. Whatever the forms of error that prevail, we who name the name of Christ are under obligation to do what is right. Difficulties we meet are no excuse to let down in our standards or our practices.

Satan ever opposes God and righteousness. He has filled the world with varied and subtle kinds of error. He presents the false in numerous forms many of which closely resemble the true. Often he makes the unreal seem real. He makes the human so attractive that you may be led to think it is divine. He so glorifies natural truth and human virtue as to cause them to be most appealing to men. If you would do right, you must do so among men who ignore man's greatest problem, the problem of sin. Satan transforms himself into an "angel of light" and does his best to lead astray every child of God. You need a salvation not only from past sins but also from false attitudes toward Christian conduct.

Regardless of what men say, it simply is not true that conduct is of no importance, that one in a state of grace need give no heed to his way of living, that it does not matter what one does if only he has faith in Christ. Those who are Christ's cannot have a light attitude toward sin, and all transgression is sin, whoever does the wrong deed. The Word of God definitely and positively stresses right conduct as well as faith. Jesus taught that we should so live as to have our good works lead men to glorify our "Father which is in heaven" (Matthew 5:16). Paul directs Titus to "affirm constantly, that they which have believed in God might be careful to maintain good works" (Titus 3:8).

No one finds it easy to live in a world where evil is held in light regard. It is not easy to practice doing good among men who ignore moral principle. It is not easy to keep free from error when we are constantly exposed to wrong teachings. It is difficult to maintain clear perceptions of right while we live among people who lack moral discernment. It is difficult to hold to high standards and to practice doing right in the midst of people who profess to be children of God but who do not do what they know to be right. No one finds it easy to take the will of God as his one guide to right living while he is in daily association with men and women who, though they say they believe the Word of God, live according to their own ideas and do as self-will prompts.

But, whatever the difficulties you meet, it is your responsibility to live so as to please God. Not the standards prevalent among men but His standard of doing right is to be yours. Whatever men think, say, or do, yours it is to maintain the kind of life worthy of a follower of Jesus. However Satan may attempt to deceive, whatever the systems devised by man, you are under obligation to do right.

God who created you and redeemed you at infinite cost justly claims from you conduct that is right in all its parts—actions, words, and thoughts. You must look to Him, not to your difficulties. If you are Christian in more than name, you are united to Him in a spiritual relationship. You have the life of God in your soul and "greater is he that is in you, than he that is in the world" (I John 4:4). The center for doing right is God, not nature, or man, or your own ideas. For everyone who is a Christian, relationship to God and doing right are inseparably one.

9

Discipline

"He openeth also their ear to discipline, and commandeth that they return from iniquity" (Job 36:10).

It is not easy to live a true Christian life. An enemy whom we cannot conquer of ourselves ever brings to us inducements to live after the world and the flesh. A world that knows not God allures us with its appeals. Our corrupt lower nature is most tenacious of life. God inclines our heart to learn the instruction of life. We must be disciplined if we are to have the singleness of heart and purpose essential to living for Christ. Depth of Christian character can come only from discipline. We must discipline ourselves in spirit and mind and body. We must learn from the disciplines of life. We must be willing subjects of God's disciplines. Discipline softens us and makes us responsive to the operation of the Spirit. However, it does not do this of itself. The grace of God with it and through it is the effective agency. It is God that opens the ear to discipline and causes the heart to respond thereto.

All that is in you of spiritual life and the fruit thereof is of God through Christ. Because Christ died on the cross you can turn from your iniquity and become holy in character and life. Neither your justification nor your growth in grace depends on anything you do. Apart from God, you have no goodness or power or strength. If you stand before God as a saved sinner, it is only through the merit of a crucified Redeemer. If you are a saint of God holy in His sight, it is solely because Christ shed His blood for you.

But you are not an inanimate creature, a mere passive object for God's grace to operate upon. You must work out what God is working in you to will and to do. You have a strong enemy to fight, an evil world to overcome, and a corrupt nature to keep in subjection to the will of God. So long as you live, you will have a battle to fight, a warfare to wage. Foes without and within assail you. To grow as a new creature in Christ Jesus, you must ever oppose the triple influence of the arch-enemy of God and your soul, the world, and your own lower nature.

Evil cannot touch your new nature, but unceasing self-discipline is necessary in dealing with the evil of your old nature. As you persistently apply such discipline, the new nature takes control over more and more area of the old nature. Either self or God rules every part of your being. The more there is of self, the less there is of God; the more there is of God the less there is of self. Mortification, or deliberate dying to self, is the price you must pay. By continual turning away from evil and denying of self, you can make possible the development of spiritual life in your soul.

God disciplines you to bring to completion the work He began in you. He disciplines you to make of you what He wants you to be, to make of you what He purposed when He redeemed you. Loving you as He does, He must correct you. If He did not do so, He would tolerate in you what is contrary to His purpose and also opposed to your own best interests. He made you His child so that you could grow to become like Him. He disciplines you to eradicate from you all that is unholy, all that is foreign to His character, He disciplines you for your good, that you may come to be a partaker of His holiness.

God disciplines you in love—perfect love, the love of a heavenly Father who sees all and knows all, yet never ceases to love. Your part is to submit completely to discipline, with the trust of a child. In that all things work together for good to those who are God's, you can rest assured that He will permit nothing that does not further your good and His purpose. The more you submit, the more fully you live and the more holy you become.

10

Discouragement

"Why art thou cast down, O my soul? and why art thou disquieted in me? hope thou in God: for I shall yet praise him for the help of his countenance" (Psalm 42:5).

The questions in this verse could be self-examining ones, asked to ascertain if discouragement has due cause. So often our disturbance of spirit is the outcome of vain imaginings. It is well, therefore, to determine whether or not disquietude has a real cause. You can ask yourself, when you feel discouraged, if there are not others who perhaps, though moping and complaining less, may not have more cause for being downcast. And you may find that actually you have more reason to be encouraged than you have to be discouraged. The questions may imply that the Psalmist was taking himself to task for having yielded to disquietude. There is a tendency in us—more pronounced in some than in others—to enjoy "feeling blue." It is well to ask yourself if you are not dishonoring God by being melancholy and dejected. You can inquire of yourself if you are not discouraging others and harming yourself by yielding to feelings of discouragement. You may question if you can give a good account before God at the bar of conscience for the disturbance you are causing. Discouragement is not natural to man. We were made for enjoyment and achievement, not for depression and inaction. "Hope springs eternal in the human breast," says the poet. The forward look, the upward glance, aspiration for higher things than we have hitherto attained, the spirit of keeping on, are the marks of a normal person. Satisfaction from effort expended, joy in having reached a chosen goal, gratification over success achieved, delight in accomplishment, even though there is yet much land to be possessed, are characteristics of a balanced personality. Sitting under a juniper tree, talking about supposed failure, and giving up the conflict, do not do honor to a human being, much less to a child of the living God.

Discouragement is a means the devil frequently uses to hinder the work of God in us and through us. In fact it is one of his favorite instruments. He knows that a downcast person is not only a poor representative of the all-powerful God but that he is also incapable of putting forth strong effort. Discouragement always weakens the hands for work. The discouraged person ceases to struggle and occupies his time and dissipates his energy in fruitless bemoaning of his lot. A bit of opposition, which all God's children have to meet, quite effectively defeats a discouraged person. It has been said with considerable truth that "the devil has many tools, but discouragement is a handle that fits them all."

The prevention of and the cure for discouragement is hope in God. One whose hope is set on God cannot be discouraged, at least not for a very long time. If you would always be encouraged, keep looking to God, not to self or to others. Nothing makes one more miserable than looking at self with its weaknesses, imperfections, failures, and sins. Nothing disturbs one more than looking to others, for never yet has man seen a man as he actually is. When you take yourself to task for your melancholy dejection, you must therefore stimulate yourself to hope in God, to set Him before the eyes of your soul, to take hold on His power and His promises, which never fail.

When you set your hope on God, you will not lack reason for praising Him. He will bring about such change in your spirit that you cannot but praise Him for His goodness and for His wonderful work in you. Hope in God is effectual in preventing and in curing discouragement. "They looked unto him, and were lightened (Psalm 34:5).

11

Doing Right

"The fruit of the Spirit is in all goodness and righteousness and truth" (Ephesians 5:9).

If you are a child of God, the Holy Spirit indwells you, producing, when He has His way, conduct that is right in all its aspects. So long as you live you will have a corrupt nature that is always at odds with the Holy Spirit. It is useless for you to try in your own strength to do right. You are, in your new nature, what God made you to be, and He created you in Christ Jesus to do good. If you have been made righteous, you will do right deeds as you allow the Holy Spirit to control, direct, and guide you. You can walk after the flesh, or your lower nature, if you will.

By your claim to be a follower of Christ, you are under obligation to do right in each and every situation. The deeds you do, speak of Him whose you say you are. When they are right, they exalt and glorify your Lord and commend Him to others. When they are not right, they dishonor your Lord and bring His cause into disrepute. Nothing so quickly and so surely hurts Christianity as Christians who do not practice honesty, truthfulness, fairness, charity, purity, self-control, and loyalty in their daily living.

God needs our service less than He needs our devotion and worship. The most and the best you can do for your Lord is to give Him one life that is right from center to circumference. What you are at heart is far more important than any service it is possible for you to render. Man looks on the outward appearance, but God looks on the heart. When the heart is right in the sight of God, when you live in humble subjection to the Holy Spirit, never quenching Him, never grieving Him, you will do right.

You cannot take self-will for your authority, you cannot live according to your own ideas, you cannot do as you think people expect you to do. You must ever seek God's standard of doing right. It is God's will that counts now in the recesses of your own conscience; it is by what God has revealed in His Word that you shall be judged in time to come. It is exceedingly dangerous to take matters of conduct lightly. Upon you, as one of Christ's representatives in this world, rests the heavy responsibility of living so as to show God to men. The only Bible many men and women read is the one they see manifested in the lives of those who call themselves Christians. If what they read be not true, grievous may be the effect in this life and terrible may be the outcome when the books are opened in the day of judgment.

When the heart is right, what you do speaks for God, in spite of mistakes and failures due to human weakness. What you are at heart rings true and carries a true message to others whether or not they show approval. There is a language of the heart which speaks more loudly than words or deeds. Sometimes those who seem to be least impressed by godly living are actually the ones who are most influenced by what they see as the issue of a heart that is right in the sight of God. Even though there are men who, like Saul of old, would destroy the pure in heart, these must admit that he who does right is more righteous than they and realize that the goodness they see manifested is of God.

12

Efficiency

"Whatsoever thy hand findeth to do, do it with thy might" (Ecclesiastes 9:10).

How efficient are you? Are you a person who is characterized by action without results? Do you do with your might what your hand finds to do but is your might poorly directed? Or do you so direct your activity that it counts toward the achievement of ends that mean something?

To be efficient, one must combine various qualities besides energy. Among these are practicality, dependability, orderliness, and concentration. Solomon advises going to the ant to consider her ways, if one would be wise. Certainly, the activity of the ant is well-directed. In contrast to the ant there is the grasshopper that hops about hither and thither but never accomplishes anything worth-while. He spends much energy, but he is not practical. He is more interested in the thrill of jumping through the air than he is in desirable outcomes that could be achieved if his energy were rightly directed. He spends time aimlessly, expending energy without accomplishing anything in particular.

So with yourself it is the mark of efficiency to choose carefully ends that are worth achieving and then to guide activity intelligently toward the achievement of those ends. Ability to get things done is not simply a matter of keeping busy but of using energy and time well. The busier some persons are, the less time they have to plan and organize their activity properly. Busyness is not, in and of itself, efficiency. You can be ever so active and yet accomplish nothing.

To get things done, use a few simple techniques. A basic one is to make a list of all the tasks you must do. Some of these will be daily tasks, others will be occasional or periodical. Determine the best time for doing each duty. Plan for mental work at times when the mind is clear and for physical tasks when the mind is less clear and the body is stocked with energy. Then estimate the amount of time that will be required for doing each task. In this way you will be able to tell easily how much you can do in a given period of time.

Work by a timetable. Outline work in advance. Plan next week's work this week, for example. Allow gaps for emergencies and unforeseen tasks. A monthly timetable or even a yearly one, flexible enough to be subject to change easily as circumstances make advisable, will give you needed direction and preparation for work in time to come.

Use your timetable after you have made it. Don't just engage in the mental exercise of making it. Use it as a guide for carrying on your work. As you complete tasks, cross them off as a record of accomplishment, thus giving yourself the psychological encouragement of seeing finished results. Review and revise your timetable frequently. Take inventory periodically—perhaps at the end of each day. Scan the schedule of the future and reschedule tasks not yet finished. Make your timetable a helpful instrument, not an inflexible thing that holds you in bondage.

Use your time to best possible advantage. Give every flying minute something to keep in store. Keeping a "log" of all the time you spend in unprofitable activities can provide you a basis for discovering ways to eliminate some of these. Time is the stuff of which life is made; the better the use you make of it, the more efficient you will be.

Develop your power of concentration. Learn to give yourself wholly to the task of the moment. There is a positive relationship between lack of concentration and inefficiency. To be efficient, you must be able to converge all your efforts toward definite accomplishment.

13

The End

"And I saw the dead, small and great, stand before God; and the books were opened: and another book was opened, which is the book of life: and the dead were judged out of those things which were written in the books, according to their works"

(Revelation 20:21).

All things have an end. This is as true of time as it is of anything else. A day comes to an end, and we go to our rest. The week has its end, bringing relief of tension built up by busy activity. Each month ends, and we turn over a leaf of the calendar to start another month with its problems and hopes. When we come to the end of a year and have to put up new calendars, we usually pause to look back a little. We tend to rush through the days, weeks, and months without stopping to look back. But when we have to put up new calendars, we are impelled to indulge in retrospection. We need such moments; they give us opportunity to ponder our ways, to consider our motives and our achievements in the light of what they ought to be.

But should we not also look ahead and realize that time itself is going to come to an end? Time marches on, but we know it will not march forever. There will be a last year, a last month, a last week, and a last day. Time moves on but it does not move apart from purpose; a goal has been set up and time is moving toward that goal, not just moving. God has set a place for it to end, and when it reaches that place, it will stop forever. Observation and experience show that time is carrying all things along toward a predetermined goal. That fact gives us purpose and direction for living. We are not "just travelling along"; we are moving toward something—an end, a last day.

Any doubt about this is quickly done away with by the Bible. It teaches that this world is on its way to a destination chosen by God. It tells us exactly what will happen at the end. If you are wise, you will consider carefully what the Bible says, for you can neither postpone nor escape the last day. Your attitude toward it will have much to do with what you do in preparation for it.

Everybody will be present on that last day. All the dead, small and great, will stand before God. Those who are living when that day comes will also be there. Men of all the ages of time will stand together in the presence of God at the end of time. Whether you want to be there or not, you will be; God, not you, has this decision to make. You may find it hard to imagine, you may think it is impossible, but God says He will assemble all men of all time in one vast congregation. What He says He will do, He does.

The last day will be a day of judgment. There will be no secrets, for God knows all, even the things you have forgotten and the things about yourself you never knew. God's judgment of men is going to be "according to their works." Salvation is by grace, but judgment will be according to works. If you are saved by grace, you will do works pleasing to God, though you be far from perfect. If you are not saved by grace, even your best works are displeasing to God. You are either a saved sinner who loves God and seeks to do His will, or you are a lost sinner who refuses to do the will of God. The difference appears in works though they be not free from sin.

The only way you can stand perfect in the end is to put your trust wholly and only in Jesus Christ. Nothing but the blood of the Son of God can blot out your sins and enable you to meet God in judgment without condemnation. If in this time of grace, you receive Him as Saviour, you will have nothing to fear in the last day, after which time shall be no more.

14

Example

"Let no man despise thy youth; but be thou an example of the believers, in word, in conversation, in charity, in spirit, in faith, in purity" (I Timothy 4:12).

Are not older people the examples in the church? Can a young person be a pattern for others to follow in becoming perfect in Christ? Can you be a model Christian? Paul tells Timothy not to let anyone look down on him because he is young, but to be "an example of the believers." Manifestly, Paul did not discount the influence of a young person.

The pride and the self-sufficiency of human nature may cause some older people to treat young people with scant consideration. Their attitude may be that "the young should be seen, not heard." But elderly men and women who have walked faithfully with the Lord for many years will appreciate and encourage the young. Whatever the attitude of adults, God can use your good example to help others, just as He can use the good example of older people to help you. It is yours so to live that your life counts for God.

To be a fit example, you must give careful heed to yourself. Don't yield to the temptation to become self-confident and careless. Don't get "cocky" over what you are or what you can do. Make certain that what you profess is actually and truly what you are at heart. It is safer to think of yourself as an example *of* the believers rather than an example *to* the believers. You are but one among a number who should be showing forth in humble dependence on God the graces of the Christian life.

In what ways can you be an example? Paul mentions six ways that take in the whole of life: speech, conduct, love, spiritual-mindedness, faith, and purity. A true example is an example on the inside and on the outside, in the unseen depths of the heart and in visible living.

You can be an example in speech. Your words betray unfailingly what you are. Let your speech be sound, your words few and sincere. You cannot influence people for God if you say more than you know and talk one way while you live another way. You can also be an example in conduct; your whole attitude as it finds expression in your deeds, can be a help and an inspiration to others. You can be an example in love—supreme love to God and love for all men. Love for one another is an outstanding mark of Christians. Every true Christian has for other men the same quality of love that God showed in giving His Son a ransom for the sins of all.

You can be spiritually minded and thus help influence your fellows to love God and the things of God instead of the world. Deep piety and real concern for spiritual values never fall flat in the effect they exert on those who see them in a consecrated child of God. You can be an example in faith, manifesting in acts that faith can be reduced to practice in daily living. If you are truly a Christian, you are a person captured by Jesus Christ, who patiently continues to do good and to strive for glory, honor, and eternal life. Finally, you can be an example in purity. You can live above all uncleanness and unholiness, maintaining a mind that is pure and thinking thoughts that are pure.

Being an example requires diligence and vigilance. It will take all that is in you, plus the grace of God. You cannot be an example if you dally with evil, making "provision for the flesh, to fulfil the lusts thereof" (Romans 13:14).

15

Failure

"I have prayed for thee, that thy faith fail not" (Luke 22:32).

"I thank God for my failures as well as for my victories, because I have learned from both of them," testified a young woman. God takes account of our striving rather than of our failures. Man, including the one who fails, is more likely to center attention upon failure. The natural tendency is to be depressed and discouraged by failure. But our failures are often God's means for bringing out the best in us. Even in this life bitter failure not infrequently has in it the beginnings of true achievement. Wendell Phillips says defeat is "nothing but the first step to something better." Someone else has said, "every failure is a step to success." The worst failure is the one from which we do not learn the lessons it can teach us.

We are built for action, and our normal desire is that everything we undertake should end in success. When instead the issue is failure, we are likely to give up in despair and discouragement. But failure is no disgrace. It is a disgrace to do less than your best to keep from failing. It is a disgrace to give up because you have failed. When you slip and fall on an icy pavement, you do not lie where you fell. Unless you are too badly hurt to do so, you get up and continue on your way, watching to avoid other patches of ice and walking carefully lest you fall again. You should do likewise when you fall figuratively.

Faith in Christ is the secret of turning failure into success. In that our Lord told Peter He had prayed for him that his faith fail not, you can assuredly believe that He prays for you also. He knows how humiliating and trying your failures are, how severely you are tempted when you fail, and how greatly you need help. He understands how you feel when you taste the bitterness of defeat. He knows that you need faith and strength to try again.

Failure is a humbling experience. A lesson you can learn from every failure is humble dependence on God. If there be one lesson above all other lessons a child of God needs to learn, it is the lesson of his own utter insufficiency. Failure shows you how weak you are. Until you realize your own weakness, you do not trust God in the way that makes it possible for Him to work in you success instead of failure. Anything that decreases your confidence in yourself and inclines you to trust more implicitly in God is good for you.

Victory and success give self-satisfaction which may easily become self-adulation, self-praise, and pride. If you always met success in what you undertook, you would likely become so lifted up in pride that God would be unable to do anything in you, for you, or through you. In the sight of God one who glories in his success is worshipping an idol, for he is putting success in the place which belongs to God.

"He that glorieth, let him glory in the Lord" (II Corinthians 10:17). If you have high standards of conduct, or achieve success in attaining them, the praise and the glory belong to God. To God belongs also the glory for any work you do for Him and the success you achieve in doing it. When failure shows you your weakness and causes you to lean wholly upon God, you can say with the Apostle Paul, "When I am weak, then am I strong" (II Corinthians 12:10). Being weak in yourself, you are strong in the grace of the Lord Jesus Christ. When failure reveals you to yourself as weak, then you will rely not on yourself but on Christ who can impart to you His own strength.

16

Faith

"Have faith in God"
(Mark 11:22).

Some people called upon a woman because they had heard that she was a woman of great faith. "Don't say that I am a woman of great faith," she said to them. "I am only one with a little faith in a great God." The life motto of Hudson Taylor was "Have faith in God." In speaking on it, he made mention of the fact that the margin says, "Have the faith of God." This, he explained, means, "Reckon on God's faith to you." Then he went on to say, "All my life has been so fickle; sometimes I could trust and sometimes I could not. But when I could not trust, then I reckoned that God would be faithful."

Faith looks to God instead of self. His disciples once asked Jesus to give them more faith. His reply to their request was, if you had faith as a grain of mustard seed, you could do wonders. It is not the size of your faith, or the amount of your faith, that counts; it is the One in whom you have faith. Andrew Murray says, "Never try to arouse faith from within. You cannot stir up faith from the depths of your heart. Leave your heart and look into the face of Christ." A tiny bit of faith placed in a faithful God works wonders whereas a mighty feeling of faith accomplishes nothing. Faith lets God do for you what you could never begin to do for yourself.

Faith gives no heed to what it sees and feels but clings to God. Anything in you that is really Christian has its origin in God through faith. By the working of the Holy Spirit in our lives, faith produces holiness, and holiness makes for the strengthening of faith. Lack of faith in God is the cause in Christian lives of unhappiness, absence of victory, and unfruitfulness. When faith is real, the soul triumphs over the flesh and all feeling. Faith brings peace with God, access to God, and puts in our soul the joy of the Lord. Faith is the only means of obtaining blessings from God.

Jesus told His disciples that, if they had faith as a grain of mustard seed, they could move mountains and that nothing would be impossible for them to do. Faith of itself cannot move mountains but by means of faith the power of God becomes operative to such removal. Through the strength and power of God in Christ, the greatest difficulty can be met effectively. "What things soever ye desire, when ye pray, believe that ye receive them, and ye shall have them" (Mark 11:24). By the miracle of faith wonders can be accomplished in your spiritual life. By faith you are justified and mountains of guilt are removed and cast into the sea of God's forgetfulness (Micah 7:19). By faith your heart can be cleansed and mountains of corruption removed. By faith you can conquer the world. By faith the fiery darts of the enemy of your soul are quenched. By faith you are crucified with Christ and yet you live. By faith you can set the Lord always before you and endure as seeing Him that is invisible, having Him continually present in thought, and this effectively removes mountains, which flee away at the presence of the Lord.

After having believed in Christ as Saviour, you have much need of faith as you go on your way. You need never hesitate to venture all on Christ, for never can your faith outstrip His bounty. When you believe, you are strong; when you doubt you weaken yourself, because by doubting you hinder, or even prevent, the working of God in you and through you. Always you can believe that whatever God says is true, however much circumstances seem to indicate the contrary. Blessed are you when you have faith, though it be little, in a great God.

17

First Things First

"Seek ye first the kingdom of God, and his righteousness; and all these things shall be added unto you" (Matthew 6:33).

In Matthew 6:26, Jesus stated three questions to the answering of which men devote the major portion of their energy. These questions are: What shall I eat? What shall I drink? What shall I wear? From the temporal point of view, these three questions are mighty important ones. You have a body which has to be sustained and maintained; you must have food and drink and clothing or your body will suffer—perhaps perish. You cannot get away from these questions; they lie at the basis of life and are the source of most of life's conflicts.

The natural man's concern is mainly for the things of time and sense—food, drink, raiment. To him the body is all-important; upon it he bestows much thought; to its welfare he gives chief attention. If man were satisfied with merely supplying the needs of the body, he would have much less difficulty than he has. Many of the conflicts of life are due to inordinate desire for things. The world's way is to lay up treasures against the time they may be needed to insure temporal welfare. Have a bank account, invest in stocks and bonds, buy houses and lands. Get one farm, and as soon as it is paid for, buy another. As the Iowa farmer said, "Buy more land to raise more corn to feed more hogs to buy more land to raise more corn to feed more hogs." The world's motto is, Take every thought for your life and get all the earthly wealth you can.

But there are more important things to think about, higher things upon which to expend energy. The life of the soul is of far greater importance than the life of the body; the things of eternity are worth infinitely more than the things of time and sense. The body lives a little while; the soul never perishes. The welfare of the soul is the one thing needful. If you put first things first, you will seek the kingdom of God and His righteousness above all else. Instead of fretting and worrying about food and raiment and being weighted down with care for the things of this world, you will have as your primary concern eternal happiness in heaven.

You must seek; you do not get things—not even eternal things—by merely wishing for them. The natural man seeks natural things. The Talmud says, "Man is born with his hands clenched; he dies with them wide open. Entering life, he desires to possess everything; leaving the world, all that he possessed has slipped away." If he departs without having laid up treasures in heaven, poor indeed will he be. The object of your seeking, the thing of first importance, is the kingdom of God. You must press toward it, you must put forth diligent effort to make sure of it, you must bend your energy toward attaining it instead of earthly things. Heaven and the righteousness of God are to have the preeminence in your thinking; they are to be first in days of youth, first every day of your life.

Whenever the things of God and the things of the world come into competition with each other, you are to give the former the preference. The promise is that you shall not lack for the things necessary to the life of the body. You get what you seek for, then besides that, you shall have food and raimant.

He who holds all in His keeping provides for the needs of those who give Him first place in their seeking. If you seek first the kingdom of God and His righteousness, God will see to it that you have as much of the things of this life as He knows is good for you. More than this you should not wish for.

18

Forward!

"Speak unto the children of Israel, that they go forward" (Exodus 14:15).

"My idea is this: ever onward. If God had intended that man should go backward, He would have given him an eye in the back of his head," says Victor Hugo. The watchword of the Christian life is, Go on. From the day the soul first meets Christ, the eye is turned toward the future. There lies all the Christian has to live for, and he presses forward to make his that which Christ made him His child to possess.

The aspirations of the Christian are always for something better. He is not content to abide in his old sins. Having caught a glimpse of Christ in His perfection, he presses on, ever seeking to realize in himself something of the beauty and the glory of the holiness of the Saviour. Through failure, disappointment, frustration, and defeat, he continually seeks to have wrought in him the sinless perfection he sees in his Lord. Though content to be his Lord's, he has in his being a divine discontentment with himself. Never again, on this side of eternity, is he satisfied to be merely what he is. Always, there are weaknesses to overcome, limitations to be delivered from, and conquests of self to be won. Looking unto God who has begun in him a work of grace, he expects Him to finish in the future the work He began. To permit of this being done, he moves forward with God.

The Christian moves forward also in the service he renders God. He shrinks not from bearing the burdens God places upon him. Whether his place be in the front or in the rear, as men view things, he owns himself, by the grace of God, equal to all a soul may. Not his to evade; he faces his God-given tasks with courage. Not his to ask, "Lord, and what shall this man do?"

He thinks not of another when the Lord appoints to him his phase of service. Not his to feel unequal to the work he knows God would have him do, for he believes God asks nothing of a child of His love that He does not provide strength sufficient to do. As a worker for God and with God, he knows that ultimate victory and success will be his, so he keeps looking to God and ever moving forward.

The hope of the Christian is in the future. He does not know what the future has in store, but he does know who has the future in His keeping. It is upon Jesus, the perfect example of faith, that the Christian keeps his eyes as he runs his course. Having taken refuge in Jesus, you have strong encouragement to grasp the hope that lies ahead. This hope, a secure and safe one, reaches into heaven itself where Jesus has entered as a forerunner on your behalf, becoming an eternal priest for you. There He appears constantly in the presence of God, pleading the efficacy of His shed blood for you, ever interceding with God for you. Thus as you came under the atonement of Christ at the time of your entrance into a state of pardon and justification, so you now have an Advocate in heaven who continues in you that state, and procures for you God's continual forgiveness. This your great High Priest will ever do until finally He brings you to where He is in the eternity of the future. Then, after time is swallowed up in eternity, there will no longer be any need for looking forward.

19

Friends

"A man that hath friends must show himself friendly" (Proverbs 18:24).

A sure way to lose the friends you have is to be otherwise than friendly. Samuel Johnson says, "A man, sir, should keep his friendships in constant repair." Shakespeare advises, "The friends thou hast, and their adoption tried, grapple them to thy soul with hoops of steel." Whether you have many friends or few, it is of much importance that you have some good friends. Friendship that is satisfying and rewarding does not just happen; you need to put forth effort to achieve it, as is true of every other good thing.

To have friends you must be friendly; you cannot be cool, reserved, and unresponsive and have others be interested in you. Friendship is a two-way affair: it involves giving as well as receiving. Make it a habit to be friendly to everyone—those you don't like as well as those you like. Never hold back and wait for the other person to show friendliness; if everybody did that, there would be no friendships. Being friendly and trying to help other people when they seem to have need, marks you as a person whom others would like to have for a friend.

Be considerate of others. Every person has his rights and his wishes. Selfishness ignores these and hurts people. Respect the property of others; no one likes to have what he owns treated in a careless manner. Be at least as careful with what belongs to another as you would be if it were yours. Consider the time of other people, for it is valuable to them. Don't make people waste time in waiting for you. Keep your promises faithfully. Follow carefully the principle that it is better not to say and do than it is to say and not do. Whatever anyone tells you in confidence, keep wholly to yourself; not to do so is one sure way to destroy a friendship.

Be cheerful at all times. Cheerfulness is a habit and can be maintained when things are not going well. No one is without troubles, and cheerfulness helps people bear their troubles. It is not easy to be cheerful when your own problems are weighing heavily upon you, but you can discipline yourself to be friendly and cheerful under all circumstances. The effort is worth all it costs.

Praise others. Look for the good in others and commend it when you see it. Everyone appreciates hearing good said about himself, if it is true. Be sincere in your praise; don't flatter, for no one likes insincerity. Even the person you flatter will suspect you of dishonest praise and lose respect for you.

Samuel Johnson also said, "If a man does not make new acquaintances as he advances through life, he will soon find himself alone." You will benefit in various ways if you take an interest in many different kinds of people. Reaching out and enlarging your circle of friends helps you to gain knowledge of people. This will serve to keep you growing. Make friends with more than one; don't be content to confine yourself to a small, exclusive group. Finally, seek unselfishly to do good to others; you cannot keep as a friend anyone whom you exploit. Friendship begun for an end will soon come to an end.

20
God

"God is love"
(I John 4:16).

A farmer once had on his barn a weather vane on the arrow of which he had printed these words from John. Someone asked him, "What do you mean by this? Do you think that God's love is as changeable as the wind?" "No," said the farmer, "I mean that whichever way the wind blows, God is still love."

What are your thoughts about God? How you think about God is important in that your thoughts determine your attitudes toward Him. What God is, is really important. Creed counts for little in and of itself. A creed may be inherited or borrowed; it may be meaningless—nothing more than a set of words and phrases to recite in services of worship; it may be held to so lightly as to have little or no effect in one's life. What counts practically are your ideas about God and your resulting attitudes toward Him.

God is real. Your ideas of Him may be most unreal and incorrect. The highest human thoughts about God are exceedingly inadequate. He is far higher and greater than any finite mind can conceive. "His greatness is unsearchable" (Psalm 145:3). If your memory serves you well, you can get a faint idea of God's greatness by going back in thought to the early days of childhood. Your father seemed to you then almost unlimited in power, able to do anything and everything. What your father seemed to you as a small child is a symbol of what God is to men. It is, of course, a faint symbol, for God is unlimited in power while the best father is still a frail and limited human being.

Your thought of God may be a childish one. It may be that you have projected into your later years the image of your father which you take to be God. In all men there is a tendency to bring God down to the human level. Because we know so little beyond the human, we are disposed to think of God as possessing the limitations and frailties common to man. Is God to you as an officer of law who is determined to keep you in order? Is He only a superior Being whom you must satisfy by means of sacrifices and ceremonies? Is He one who keeps records of your many misdeeds, with the intention of taking you to account for them? Is He one who is as variable as yourself who may be for you today and against you tomorrow? Is He a Being who, though He forgives your sins, never forgets that you sinned against Him?

God is far exalted above our human conceptions. "God is a Spirit" (John 4:24). If you would have the right idea of Him, you must think of Him as the infinite, personal, self-existent, absolute, unchangeable, ever-present, all-powerful, all-knowing Spirit. God has no body; we must not think of Him in terms of flesh.

You must think of Him in terms of the declaration of the only begotten Son, "which is in the bosom of the Father" (John 1:18). The Son has told us that "God is love," that He so loved the world that He gave His best. He loves us as only a perfect Father can. And this perfect heavenly Father says to all who put their trust in Him, "Can a woman forget her sucking child, that she should not have compassion on the son of her womb? yea, they may forget, yet will I not forget thee. Behold, I have graven thee upon the palms of my hands. . . Yea, I have loved thee with an everlasting love" (Isaiah 49:15, 16; Jeremiah 31:3).

21

Gossip

"Death and life are in the power of the tongue"
(Proverbs 18:21).

Did you ever kill a person? Your reaction to this question may be emphatically negative, but revolvers and poison are not the sole means of destruction. Words sometimes kill. No one knows how many suicides are actually murders. When a person takes his life because false statements are being made about him, the one who started the gossip may be the individual who is really responsible for the death. Many an accident in which a life or lives are snuffed out occurs when nerves are tense, minds disturbed, and spirits wrought up because someone gossiped. Physical destruction is not the only form of destruction wrought by words. Friendships are broken, reputations ruined, characters wrecked, energy sapped, intentions frustrated, hopes killed, by malicious talk.

Why do people spread rumors? For one thing, they want excitement. Ordinary life is too tame and uneventful. Facts do not give sufficient stimulation to satisfy them. Gossip stirs things up, making for exciting change. Then there is the desire for attention. In us is something that enjoys being in the limelight. We like to be thought intelligent. The sad fact is that an empty brain and a tattling tongue usually go together. The peddler of gossip recites items of news or scandal with the purpose of attracting attention to himself, often with little or no thought of the effect on the person about whom he talks.

Desire for prestige is another motivating factor back of gossip. The talebearer assumes consciously or unconsciously that he knows something others do not know. This gives him a feeling of superiority. Typically, those given to gossip have inferiority complexes, and gossiping is a means they use to become dominant over listeners. Feelings of insecurity cause people to gossip. The ruiner of reputations may be an insecure person who feels inability to carry on conversation, so he tries to compensate by saying something of startling nature. He may feel insecure socially, and so he does what he can to pull down the socially accepted. Worst of all, he may be insecure morally. His believing the worst about others and his resultant gossiping may be his means for trying to escape the guilt he feels in his own conscience.

You must come to know yourself if you would be free from the crime of killing people and ruining lives by gossip. Whenever you find yourself taking delight in listening to an unflattering story about someone, examine yourself. Ask yourself if you are seeking the limelight or if you desire excitement. When you give way to the urge to repeat a rumor you have heard, search your heart to determine the secret guilt you are trying to hide.

You must not ignore the serious nature of gossip. To pass it by with the thought that "people will talk, so let them talk" is not the thing to do. If you are the one talked about, you can afford to pay little heed, for that is likely the best way to deal with it. But if you are the gossiper, or the willing listener to gossip, you must face the facts, however unpleasant they may be. Invariably, we talk about, or listen eagerly to things that interest us. Therefore, when you are a participator, active or passive, in gossip, every word is a reflection on yourself. Listening to or repeating gossip is always a personal confession of excessive desire for attention, of malice, of moral weakness, or of lack of spirituality.

22

Guidance

"And the Lord shall guide thee continually"
(Isaiah 58:11).

It would be something great if an angel should guide you, but here it is said that the Lord Himself shall guide. God does not let you in your pilgrimage through this world to the guidance of a lesser being than Himself. He goes on before to lead you in the right way. You may not always realize that He is guiding but you may be most certain that He will never forsake you. "I will never leave thee nor forsake thee," is His sure word to you. Always He is better to you than you hoped He would be. Always the fears that tormented you prove to be groundless. The storms and the trials that beset you bring home to you the fact that the Lord is ever near.

The statement is emphatic—the Lord *shall* guide you. If it were *will,* the meaning expressed would be simple futurity. *Shall* makes the statement a declaration of determination, most certain, most positive. There is not the least possibility but that the Lord will guide now, tomorrow, and as long as guidance is needed. Whatever comes, He "shall guide" you. Through pain, joy, suffering, good, evil, failure, victory, pleasant, unpleasant, agreeable, disagreeable, everything and anything, "the Lord shall guide thee." You have only to follow Him through thick and thin, desired and undesired, the understood and the perplexing, the known and the unknown. The Lord is bound to guide you; He is not as a human being who may be swerved from a course He has chosen to take. He always completes what He begins to do.

"The Lord shall guide thee continually." The word is not *constantly* which means "frequently or closely repeated." If the Lord led you constantly, there would be periods of time in which

He was not guiding, interspersed with periods during which He was guiding. Guiding you *continually,* He guides you "without interruption," that is, there is never a period of time—even a moment—when He is not guiding you. He does not guide you sometimes but perpetually—without cessation. He does not leave you occasionally to your own understanding and devices, to wander and to blunder, but you are all the time under His guidance.

Left to your own way for but an instant, you are likely to get yourself into serious difficulty. As Augustine said of himself, so you can say that to yourself you are nothing but a guide to your own downfall. Your way is not in yourself (Jeremiah 10:23). The wisdom you have is utterly inadequate for coping with the issues of living. You are finite in knowledge; however much you may learn, there will be oceans of truth of which you will always be ignorant. You lack understanding; human insight is never perfect.

"The Lord shall guide thee continually." You have no problems that are insoluble to God. You have no questions He cannot answer. There are no difficult situations out of which He is unable to deliver you. Never will you go wrong when you go in the company of God. Like Enoch, walk with God and you walk the road to heaven and unspeakable glory. When you walk with God, you have infallible wisdom to direct you, infinite knowledge to shield you, perfect understanding to enlighten you, immutable love to comfort you, and everlasting power to defend you. The Lord's hand to guide is better than any human aid, for it upholds while it guides.

23

Humility

"Be clothed with humility: for God resisteth the proud, and giveth grace to the humble"
(I Peter 5:5).

Humility, the most difficult virtue, is the root of all heavenly virtues. It is the humble, contrite heart that God looks upon in merciful favor. It is he who humbles himself that God exalts. God delights in the humble person and promises many things to him. From him who is truly humble He holds back no blessing. If you would be under the blessing of God and if you would live in harmonious relations with your fellowman, you must cultivate humility.

You will never be humble except as you do cultivate this grace. Only you can humble yourself; only you can cloth your spirit with humility. The way to cultivate humility is to look to Christ. Consider Him who, though equal with God, took upon Himself the form of a slave and served the eternal interests of unworthy human beings. Never has the world seen a comparable example of humility. You cannot become humble by trying to be humble, for the instant you feel you are humble you will not be so. The more you try, the less humble you will be. The true way to keep humble, it has been said, is to keep "face to face with the humbling facts and the great realities, to stand against some great nature." There is no nature greater than Christ's; you cannot but be humble if you have His vision of God, of man, and of self.

The spirit of true humility will be yours when you, like the publican of whom Jesus told, see yourself as a defiled sinner, utterly unworthy even to approach God, and cast yourself upon Him for mercy. "God be merciful to me a sinner," will then be your prayer as you seek pardon, forgiveness, and grace. You will advertise no merits as did the proud Pharisee. You will, rather, accuse yourself, attempting no justification of yourself or your past. What you need and want will be the undeserved mercy of God. When you are really aware of this need, your humility will be such as to require few words for expressing that need. Seeing yourself thus as God sees you, you cannot think highly of yourself.

Moreover, you have a check on high thoughts of yourself when you consider men. If you value the good in others at its real worth, if you know your lacks, you will see many who are deserving of more honor than you. Every person you meet has personal merits you do not have. Every person has probably accomplished some things you have not—perhaps could not—accomplish with the powers you have. Every person is more worthy than you in respect to some quality of character. Instead of being proud that you have so much, you have abundant reason for being humble that there are so many superior to you.

Let your mind, conduct, and whole person be clothed with humility. It is the most beautiful garb you can wear. It will make obedience and duty easy and pleasant. It will water the plant of love; a proud spirit is destructive of Christian love; there is no greater enemy to peace among Christians than pride. When you do things in pride to show off, to attract attention to yourself, to attain preeminence among your fellows, you destroy Christian love and kindle unchristian feeling.

If you be proud and disobedient, God will set Himself against you, to oppose and destroy you. "He resisteth the proud." His judgments are coming upon all men, beginning "at the house of God." His power is omnipotent and can easily pull you down if you are proud, or exalt you if you are humble. He will certainly do either, in this life if He sees it is best for you, or at the last day.

24

Intercession

"He saw that there was no man, and wondered that there was no intercessor"

(Isaiah 59:16).

There's no weapon so mighty
As the intercessors bear;
Nor a broader field of service
Than the ministry of prayer.

There is desperate need for the special ministry of intercessory prayer. Intercession means "a coming between." It is standing in the gap between God and men by prayer, to turn away God's wrath. It is a warfare against the hosts of evil.

Probably there is no field which has so few workers as this one. Three facts may account for the dearth: first, it is a ministry which seldom brings the worker to the fore where he can be seen of men; second, it is difficult work; third, not many people realize what a glorious privilege it is to engage in this tremendously important ministry. Adolph Saphir, an eminent Hebrew Christian leader emphasized its importance in these words: "If I were to live my life over again I would spend less time in service and more in prayer."

Intercessory prayer is truly a warfare and every intercessor is a warrior. This means striving, battling, overcoming determined opposition. Every prayer concerns at least three beings: he who prays, God to whom he prays, and Satan whose relentless purpose it is to hinder prayer in every way possible. No person can engage in intercessory prayer without meeting and conquering tremendous difficulties. Charles G. Finney says, "I am convinced that nothing is so rarely attained as a praying heart."

Grand and glorious is the privilege of engaging in the ministry of intercessory prayer. To stand in the breach between God and men, to intercede with God in behalf of men, to be engaged in the Lord's battle against the hosts of evil, to plead His own promises to men, to uphold His righteousness in dealing with men, to beseech Him to be merciful for the sake of Jesus who gave His life for the lost—these are, indeed, things that angels might well desire to do.

One who engages in intercessory prayer is doing the same work that the ascended Lord is doing, for "He ever liveth to make intercession" for those for whom He died the death of the cross. As He interceded for Peter before He went back to heaven, so He continues to intercede before the throne, pleading the merit of His shed blood to turn away the wrath and eternal destruction deserved by men.

While Christ intercedes for men in heaven, the Holy Spirit intercedes for those who pray, in their hearts. "We know not what we should pray for as we ought." So the Spirit enlightens us, teaches us what to pray for, stimulates praying graces, comforts and encourages us in our fears, and helps us overcome opposition. We cannot pray effectually without the aid of the Spirit to dictate our requests and to draw up our pleas for us. But that aid is ours, for "the Spirit also helpeth our infirmities" (Romans 8:26). "Let us therefore come boldly unto the throne of grace" in intercessory prayer. Prayer is work, but prayer works —far beyond the comprehension of human minds.

25

Knowing Right and Wrong

"Woe unto them that call evil good, and good evil" (Isaiah 5:20).

Ever since man fell into sin, he has been prone to take evil for good and good for evil. As a believer in Christ, you have yet a corrupt nature that inclines you to do this. You need, therefore, to use every available means for ascertaining what is right and what is wrong. Except as you do, you will be led astray before you know it.

One means is your intelligence and reason. God endowed you with mental powers and He expects you to use them. You are not to be as a dumb brute that has no understanding. God's call is, "Come now, and let us reason together" (Isaiah 1:18), and His admonition is, "Ponder the path of thy feet, and let all thy ways be established" (Proverbs 4:26). You need not have complete understanding of everything to know the difference between right and wrong. If you are normal in mental life, you can give careful, thoughtful attention to moral matters.

But reason, being perverted by sin, is not a perfect guide to what is right. You need only observe mankind in general and your own experience in particular to realize that reason is darkened and limited in its perception of what is right. By Adam's sin and its effect on your nature and by your own sins, the ruin of your being is so great that "reason is obscured, especially in practical matters, the will is made obdurate to evil, good actions become more difficult and concupiscence more impetuous." You can not, therefore, rely too much on reason.

A second means whereby you can distinguish between right and wrong is conscience. It is a knowing of what is right or wrong in relation to the moral standard or law: it is not the ground of the moral law but the perception of its decrees. The important fact about conscience is judgment; it judges you, excusing or not excusing you. Decisions made without considering what is right or wrong involve judging afterward; if you weigh matters before deciding, conscience gives warning judgment beforehand of the moral quality of what is being considered. However, conscience, like reason, is the victim of our sinful nature and therefore not infallible. You cannot therefore trust it fully.

The only means upon which you can place complete reliance is the teachings of the Word of God and the guidance of the Holy Spirit. You are insufficient of yourself to know the difference between right and wrong, but you have God's oft-repeated promise of guidance. Your "ears shall hear a word behind thee, saying, This is the way, walk ye in it, when ye turn to the right hand, and when ye turn to the left" (Isaiah 30:21). The Holy Spirit guides in harmony with the teachings of the written Word so that you need not be ignorant of what is right.

In general, the principles of the Word are sufficient to indicate what is right and to warn against what is wrong. When further need exists, the Holy Spirit illuminates the Word, quickens the conscience, and gives detailed directions. Jesus, speaking of the Holy Spirit, said, He will "bring all things to your remembrance, whatsoever I have said unto you" (John 14:26), and "He will guide you into all truth" (John 16:13). Always, the Spirit guides in harmony with the written Word.

You are to walk circumspectly, not as a senseless being; you are to be wise, understanding what the will of the Lord is (Ephesians 5:15–17). You are under heavy obligation to be most careful in respect to right and wrong. You are to live soberly and righteously, whatever others may do or not do. Always, you should do your very best to know what is right and what is wrong and to do the right.

26

Leadership

"If the blind lead the blind, both shall fall into the ditch" (Matthew 15:14).

Among men there are always leaders. In any group of two or more people, one person is bound to lead. The leadership may pass from one to another in accordance with the qualifications of this, that, or the other person for leading in connection with the particular matter at hand; but there will always be a leader. Probably every person is a leader at some time or other, in relation to some thing or other. However, it is manifest to everyday observation that some individuals are better qualified than others to be leaders of their fellows. If it is yours to lead, you do not well to shirk the responsibility of leading; if your place is that of a follower, be content to follow well. In thus doing, you will be upholding the hands of the leader and so helping along in the common cause. Were there no followers, there could be no leading.

No person can lead who does not have a personal interest in those he leads. By superior power of personality, by force of some kind or other, by dint of greater knowledge, or by some other means, one may drive men, compelling them to do what he wants them to do. But he cannot lead those he does not love. Domination over people is not leadership. Domination is not known in the kingdom of God. Love is the ruling force there, first, last, and always—from God the Leader of all down to the lowest leader.

Instead of driving his men, the true leader coaches them. To lead men, one must be on higher ground. However, the true leader is humble, not characterized by feelings of superiority. His one desire and purpose is to achieve the end set by the group.

Always, for him the work to be done is more important than his part in the work. So, as a wise coach does, he seeks to weld into a composite body all the members of the group, including himself. He sees that each individual knows what he is to do, and he helps each one to do well his particular phase of the common task. This means that, instead of counting on his authority, the good leader gets the good will and the voluntary cooperation of every one in the group.

The real leader makes little use of the perpendicular pronoun; instead of "I" he makes it "we." Thus he leads his followers into a real sense of responsibility for doing their best in all that is to be done. It is not the leader's work; it is the work of the group, to be done by the group working as a unit, and any rewards that come will be rewards to the group. Thus, instead of keeping his followers guessing and fearful, the good leader arouses their enthusiasm. He stimulates each to do the best he can, encourages his efforts, and works along with the entire group, helping wherever possible. He is a helper in a common cause, not a boss.

In any well-led group, a spirit of good fellowship and healthy confidence are present. The leader enters into the hopes and the plans of each member. He inspires confidence, for he has so thought through in advance the lines of work that each person in the group cannot but believe he knows where he is going and how he will get there. Thus they can trust him to get them to the right place.

27

Levels of Living

"Man that is in honor, and understandeth not, is like the beasts that perish"

(Psalm 49:20).

A human being is a spirit existing in a body. As a human being, you are the creature whose body is supreme among all material bodies; you are the being who is only "a little lower than the angels"; you are the one whom God has crowned with glory and honor. You are not divine, you are not angelic, you are not bestial, but human. You are a spirit that came from God to exist for a time in a body and is destined, depending on your choice, to return to Him to live forever with Him in eternal glory.

While you are in this body, you can live on the animal level, if you so desire. You have appetites, and inclinations such as animals have. The standard for living as an animal is purely physical—the satisfying of the propensities and inclinations of the body. The glory of animal living is brute strength; its goal is the gratification of physical needs. In every age there are human beings who act and live like animals.

You can choose to live on the human level. Though you have powers limited by weakness and corrupted by sin, you are a human being. Your natural tendencies are neither manifestations of iniquity nor evidences of holiness. They are human equipment that you can use to ascend to lofty heights or to descend to very low depths. Your power to will is a source of truly marvelous and most challenging possibilities. In every age there are men and women who live as human beings.

You can live on the divine level, if you will. God gave man originally a nature like His own; He created man in His own image. He made you a living self which is not entirely devoid of this image even if it is greatly marred by sin. You can express this self in terms of the life of God which, though it was lost through sin, can be restored to your soul through the grace of the Lord Jesus Christ. At the end of time, God is going to judge you for the way in which you have expressed this self. His standard for judging will be the moral law He implanted in your being, the teachings of His written Word, and your faith in Jesus Christ with its outcome within you of the life of Christ. God and all the privileges of His wonderful grace are yours when you live on the divine level. In every age there are human beings who live as saints of God.

If you choose to live on the animal level, you will receive help so to live. The joy and the exhilaration of pure animal spirits functioning normally is a boon to living on this level. However, your nature will not allow you to be long content with such a manner of life. It is all right at times, but you are a moral and spiritual being whose longings cannot be satisfied forever in animal ways. If you choose to live on the human level, much help will be given you. Forces within yourself will lend you aid, many people will help you, and various social organizations will provide assistance. But all human help—your own and every other—is weak, limited and insufficient at best. "The way of man is not in himself: it is not in man that walketh to direct his steps" (Jeremiah 10:23).

If you choose to live on the divine level, you will have real assistance, for you will have the help of Him whose strength never fails. In the words of Augustine, "Thy omnipotency is not far from us even when we are far from thee." God is "a very present help" not only in times of trouble but at all times. The great limitless, sufficiency of the all-powerful God is yours when you choose to walk the way of life with Him.

28

Life and Death

"I know whom I have believed, and am persuaded that he is able to keep that which I have committed unto him against that day"
(II Timothy 1:12).

These are the words of the aged Paul. About thirty years before he wrote them, he had met Christ on the road to Damascus. Between the time of this meeting and the day he wrote the words, he had been telling men all over the Roman world the glorious good news of salvation through our Saviour Jesus Christ. When he wrote the words, he was in a dark, dirty, damp prison awaiting his sentence, which he knew would be death.

It is human to cling to life and to fear death. But through what He accomplished for us when He died on the cross, Jesus Christ has done away with death. Paul knew that he was soon to die. From the human point of view, he had reason for sadness and fear. But he was not looking at the future from the human point of view. Instead of clinging to life and fearing death, he was looking forward to death.

Why could Paul face death thus? Because he knew that it would free him from all the sufferings and limitations of bodily existence. He had believed on Christ who had abolished death, therefore the death of the body would be for him only a passing from earth and its sorrows to the blessedness of the eternal world. As Christ destroyed the power of death when He died, so He gave His followers assurance of everlasting life by rising from the dead. Because He arose, those who are His shall also arise from the dead to live forever with Him. This was Paul's strongly assured confidence.

Paul had no reason to fear, for Christ whom he had served

these many years had never let him down. He had supreme confidence that the Lord, in whom he had trusted and whom he had found sufficient for all things, was able to keep his soul in safety until he reached his eternal home in heaven. Years before, after he had met Christ, Paul had committed his life into the care and keeping of the Lord. Soon now, men would put him to death, but he knew that his life would be restored to him, gloriously improved, the moment his spirit passed from earth to heaven.

Did you ever ask yourself how you would feel and what you would do if you knew that you had only one more day to live? Maybe you do not like to think about such things. Typically, young people are so interested in living that they do not care to think about dying. Most who are young have many years of life ahead of them. But you can never be sure how long you will live. Not one of us knows what a day will bring forth. Certain it is, the old must die, but the young may die at any moment.

Are you going to heaven when you die? For those who refuse to believe on Christ, physical death means the beginning of everlasting suffering and sorrow. But anyone who really trusts the Lord can confidently say with Paul, "I know," "I am persuaded" that my soul is safe in the keeping of the Lord for time and for eternity.

29

A Life for God

"For the love of Christ constraineth us; because we thus judge, that if one died for all,...that they which live should not henceforth live unto themselves, but unto him which died for them, and rose again"

(II Corinthians 5:14, 15).

The heavenly vision Paul saw on the Damascus road changed entirely his life. This highly educated man was a puzzle to his fellow Jews. That one so well versed in the teachings of Moses as he should be devoted to a Man whom His own people had deemed worthy of death was completely beyond their comprehension. To them this great scholar and outstanding thinker lived a very strange and peculiar life.

It was a life strange and peculiar also to his fellow Christians. None gave themselves as did he so entirely to the service of the Lord that nothing had any weight with him but the will of God and faithfulness to Him. This devotion resulted in the loss of all. They could not understand his determination and his actions when he had to suffer so much. He would preach one day and be in prison the next. He kept on preaching even when stricken down in supposed death. Whatever happened to him, he went on preaching and suffering, counting no conditions, no obstacles, as reasons for ceasing. The explanation of this life was that God had revealed to Paul the place He would have him fill in the purpose He has for the world.

God's carrying out of this purpose involves each one of us. We fail Him if we do not fill the place He has for us. If we would qualify for that place, we must surrender ourselves wholly to God, whatever the cost, whatever we may meet. It is possible to live a God-planned life—a life in which God has first place and through which God works day by day. God has a plan for every life. The plan originates with Him. It allows for no compromise or turning aside; the method of its outworking must be God's, and God's alone.

Every created thing shows that God's method of working is from the center outward. When we ignore this method, we frustrate God's plan and fail. To be in harmony with this method means that God must be in complete control at the center of our being, that our life must be entirely and unreservedly in God's hands. To work out His plan, God must have the complete use of every power of our being, of all the members of our body, of everything we are and have. God who plans is the only One who can work out the plan. Multitudes of human beings have proved this to their own sorrow; man's efforts always end in terrible failure.

You cannot afford to limit God and fail to fulfil the glorious plan He has for you. Let it not be yours to be so much occupied with yourself and your own little plans and your petty interests that you are oblivious to the purpose of God. May the vision of His purpose for the lost world overshadow your whole life as it did the Apostle Paul's. Not to respond to it will mean loss in your own soul. The Spirit speaks, calling you to surrender to God that He may work in you as He will what He wills.

Do not relegate the vision God gives you to an out-of-the-way place in your thinking. Do not despise the challenge God presents. Yield to Him, respond with all that is in you, and you will help bring nearer the consummation of all things when God shall be all in all. You were born into the world for such a time as you now live in and you have the privilege of being used of God. You were redeemed in the precious blood of Christ that you might be used of God in bringing others to Him.

30

Love to God

"Take diligent heed...to love the Lord your God" (Joshua 22:5).

The children of Israel were commanded to love the Lord their God with all their powers (Deuteronomy 6:5). Jesus said this is the first and greatest of all the commandments (Matthew 22:38). Love is the leading affection, the rest and the satisfaction of the soul, and our love is to go out to God above all else. Supreme love to God is the first and greatest commandment because it is the foundation of all the rest. When the whole being of man is concentrated to love God more than anything else, he renders obedience to all the other commandments.

Loving God supremely solves all problems concerning men's relations to each other. When God has first place in the affections, love to man follows. Where love prevails, difficulties involved in getting along with people are fewer in number and relatively easy to solve. All evil passion vanishes before supreme love to God. Questions of right and wrong are quickly settled in the light of such love.

Love always finds expression in acts. A love that is content merely with a light feeling in the region of the heart or with expression in words is not really love. Any being who loves another being is impelled by his affection to do things on behalf of the one he loves. No sacrifice is too great, no burden is too heavy, no expense is too costly, if it but serve the best interests and the pleasure of the object of his affection.

Because of the importance of love to God, you may well inquire, what are the marks of that love? In answer to the question, the following seven marks are tests which may be used to determine the reality of your love: First, obedience to God. Love delights to satisfy the heart of the one loved. Nothing you can do pleases God so much as loving, humble obedience to all His known will. Second, love to man. "He that loveth not his brother whom he hath seen, how can he love God whom he hath not seen?" (I John 4:20). You make a mockery of your professed love to God if you do not truly love your fellowmen—the unlovely as well as the lovely.

Third, the general bend and turn of your thoughts when they are not occupied with the necessary affairs of daily life. Does God have first place in your thoughts? Do your thoughts, when not otherwise occupied, turn naturally toward Him? Compare the place God has in your thoughts with that held by a dearly loved human being. Fourth, your disposition toward prayer and the study of God's Word. Love disposes you to commune with one for whom you have strong affection; you find joy in reading messages from such a one. If you love God as you ought, can you spend the major portion of your time before the radio, the television set, in reading frothy magazines and unedifying books, or in superficial association with other people?

Fifth, your attitude toward God's Son, Jesus Christ. Was He merely a good man? Was He one who did no more than set us a perfect example? Or, was He God's only begotten Son who lived the life of God and died the death of God on your behalf? Is He not only our Saviour but also the Lord and Master of your life and your coming King whom you are looking forward to seeing? Sixth, your attitude toward the present world. If you love the world, you do not love God. If you hanker after the things of the world, whatever love you have for God is weak. Seventh, your interest in the advancement of the kingdom of God. Are you living day by day for God, letting your light shine for Him? Do you desire to see souls brought to Him? Are you concerned about carrying the message of His love to the lost of earth? Love for God means love for souls for whom His Son, in love, gave His life.

31

Manners

"Be courteous"
(I Peter 3:8).

A father thus advised his son: "My boy, treat everybody with politeness even those who are rude to you. Remember, you show courtesy to others, not because they are gentlemen but because you are one."

Are you often unmindful of the rights of others? Do you fail to express gratitude to those who do favors for you? Are you gracious to strangers but forever growling at those who are near and dear to you? Are you careful of your own possessions but careless of the belongings of others? Do you ever borrow and fail to return? Do you treat tradesmen and salespeople as the small scum of the earth?

We live in a rapid age, an age of rapid eating, rapid working, rapid thinking, rapid travel, rapid everything. Our forefathers traveled in ox carts and horse-drawn vehicles, making their ten or fifty miles a day. Today we travel in automobiles, stream-lined trains, and transcontinental planes, going hundreds and thousands of miles a day. Things move so fast that we are in danger of being too busy to appreciate the little courtesies of life.

Maybe you think you have no time for good manners, that they belong to an age in which things did not move so rapidly. You may agree with some who say that politeness is a bit "sissy." You may have been told that politeness is not a Christian virtue, that charity is Christian, but politeness belongs to the world of non-Christians. Or you may think that politeness is akin to hypocrisy, that it is a pretense, a showing of feelings that are not genuine.

Far from being "sissy," politeness is actually strength under control. It is strength held in check, out of consideration for the rights or the benefits of others. Instead of selfishly taking what it can get, politeness stands aside and allows others to obtain what they need or want. Worldly politeness consists primarily in showing deference to those to whom it is expedient to manifest consideration. But there is such a thing as Christian politeness. This is founded on something altogether different from the desire to gain favor. Basically, it is doing to others what you would have them do to you. It shuns for others what is distaseful to self. It does the kindest thing in the kindest way, which is the essence of true politeness. Christians are polite to those who can do nothing, or will do nothing, for them. Essentially, politeness is an expression of Christian charity. Christians are polite because of loving consideration for those for whom Christ died.

False politeness is tainted with hypocrisy. True politeness is permeated through and through with love for fellowmen. Mere good manners often are a disguise for cruel insincerity. Genuine good manners are a manifestation of a real desire to help others along life's road, saving them from things that jar and jolt.

You have to live with others. Politeness is the oil that makes possible the smooth operation of group living. It is needed more, rather than less, in a rapid age. Because movement is fast, there is need for being more careful not to collide with the interests of others. Because human selfishness appears in so many forms, you need to manifest, as an outcome of deep, true love of your fellows, a politeness that is of the heart, good manners that are born in the soul.

Are you polite everywhere, to everybody, at all times, under all circumstances? How are your manners? Do they commend or condemn your profession?

32

Missionary Vision

"My meat is to do the will of him that sent me, and to finish his work" (John 4:34).

What is missionary vision? How can you get it? Missionary vision involves more than merely looking upon the fields which are white unto harvest. William Carey said that his call to preach the gospel to those in the regions beyond was an open Bible and a map of the world. But one can see the need of the world and yet be without missionary vision. Many have looked upon this need and gone forth to engage in social work, economic betterment, and medical service. All of these, valuable as they may be as parts of the missionary enterprise, can be done by people who have no vision for God and souls. Human aims and human effort, however exalted and worthy they may be in and of themselves, are not elements in missionary vision.

On the other hand, it is not necessary that one have a visit from angels in order to have missionary vision. This vision is the ability to see with the eyes of mind and heart our God in His glory, to get His view of the world, to understand something of His purpose, to get a glimpse of His plan, and to gain a conception of His provision for the accomplishment of His plan. Missionary vision is a spiritual vision, spiritually imparted. Only the Holy Spirit can give true missionary vision.

Jesus did tell His disciples to lift up their eyes and look upon the harvest fields which were white, ready for reaping. Vision involves more than looking with the physical eyes. A Spirit-opened heart must see the value of the harvest and the purpose and plan of God for gathering in the harvest. Missionary vision which is the basis and the support of missionary passion comes, not from seeing the fields after the fashion of man. It comes from knowing God, as our Lord knew Him, knowing the sovereign God who has a goal for the world, the loving, compassionate God who is "not willing that any should perish, but that all should come to repentance" (II Peter 3:9).

You will never possess the vision, you will never see the fields white to harvest until you see God with the eyes of your heart and the sight of faith. Isaiah's account of his vision begins with the words "I saw the Lord." After he had seen the Lord "high and lifted up" he could then see his part in God's plan. Only after he had seen the Lord could he see the people's need, the work to be done, his own powerlessness, and God's way for him. Now as in Isaiah's time, the real vision is the Spirit-given sight that beholds God, His work, and His goal.

In wonderful grace, God has not only redeemed your soul but He also calls you to be a worker together with Him as He carries out His purpose for bringing men into His eternal kingdom. His plan of the ages is moving onward toward its ultimate consummation. Jesus said, "My meat is to do the will of him that sent me, and to finish his work." For Him, the doing of the Father's will included Calvary, but He never flinched from His task. Now, through the Holy Spirit, He is imparting His vision and calling His children to serve and to suffer with Him in doing the Father's work.

To be missionary-minded is to be Christ-minded; to be Christ-minded is to be missionary-minded and possessed by the missionary vision. This will mean Christ's living in you, through you, and by you. His passion for the world and His compassion for lost men will be yours also. Then will your Christ-possessed, Christ-controlled heart cry with David Livingstone, "My Jesus, my King, my Life, my all, I dedicate my whole self to Thee." And then shall your Lord "see of the travail of his soul, and shall be satisfied" (Isaiah 53:11).

33

Money

"The love of money is the root of all evil"
(I Timothy 6:10).

Money itself is neither good nor bad. In this world it is necessary and useful. So long as it is kept in its proper place, it serves good and commendable purposes. Its proper place is that of a servant to ends higher than itself. Paul does not condemn money; he does not consider the possession of money to be wrong. He admonishes Timothy to be constant in charging those that are rich not to put their trust in their money but to keep themselves from the love of their riches and the pride that the human heart is prone to take in riches. Instead, they are to trust "in the living God, who giveth us richly all things to enjoy" (I Timothy 6:17). He recognized that riches can become the master of life.

Money can be a good servant. Used as a gift from God, in dependence upon Him, in His fear and with an eye single to His glory, the money you have, be it little or much, can be a source of blessing to others and to yourself. God gives us "richly all things to enjoy," not to own forever but to use for good and worthy purposes. By sharing with others less fortunate than ourselves, we express love. When we give in love, two are blessed, him who receives and him who gives. And the blessing depends not upon the amount given but the spirit in which it is given. A little truly shared means far more than a large amount doled out in a superior, unloving manner.

While money rightly used is a good servant, it is a hard master when love of it takes possession of the heart. God never intended that it be man's master. However, so great is the corruption of the human heart, so prone are we to set our affection upon the visible and the temporal instead of the unseen and spiritual, that desire for money and for the things we can acquire with money can easily become inordinate. Such desire crowds out good impulses, drowns the voice of conscience, crushes noble ambitions, and makes one inhuman. Men possessed by avarice and greed become monsters of cruelty who make countless thousands suffer intensely. When passion for gain takes a firm hold upon a man he will stoop to almost any crime that seems likely to make him richer.

We came into this world without anything, and we shall leave it as empty-handed as we came. There is but one answer to the question often asked when a man dies; how much did he leave? That answer is, All he had. There are no pockets in a shroud, there are no strong boxes in a tomb, there are no vaults in heaven for the storage of earthly riches.

In days of youth, aspirations are, typically, high and noble. The young person is inclined to be generous in the use of his money and without extreme desire to amass wealth. But as the stern realities of life are thrust upon him, he faces the danger of losing the lofty visions of youth. You must remember that God expects you to be content with receiving what you need while you are in this world. Riches have a way of grabbing at human hearts and tempting man to turn away from God. Only as you allow the Holy Spirit to control you, can you be kept free from selfish desires and destructive affections. You cannot love Christ and love money at the same time. If you are wise, you will set your affection upon Him and you will store up your treasures in heaven.

34

The Two Natures

"For the flesh lusteth against the Spirit, and the Spirit against the flesh: and these are contrary the one to the other; so that ye cannot do the things that ye would" (Galatians 5:17).

Every Christian is conscious that there are two tendencies within him. Part of him wants to do the will of God, part of him wants to serve self; part of him longs for the rest of the promised land, part of him lusts for the leeks and garlic of Egypt; part of him grasps Christ, part of him grips the world. There is a law which pulls him sinward while at the same time another law pulls him Christward. The Scriptural explanation is that every believer has two natures: the sinful, fleshly nature, and the spiritual, Christ nature.

These words of Ruth Paxson emphasize the truth that is clearly unfolded in I John 1:18. "Any person, however long he may have been a Christian, who says he has no sin and is entirely freed from his old nature deceives himself. He deceives no one else, least of all those who associate with him in daily life, and most assuredly he does not deceive God. Any one of us can get a good view of 'himself' if he will only picture to himself the lowest, meanest, vilest human being imaginable. That is God's view of us—this self, this sinful flesh which He sentenced to death on the cross. We dearly love this self and cling to it most tenaciously. But the sentence of death was paid in full in our Lord who died carrying our sinful flesh with Him."

The existence in us of these two natures so opposed to each other makes inevitably for conflict. It is the old, old conflict between Satan and God, with the being of the Christian as the place of battle. Paul vividly describes the conflict in the seventh chapter of Romans. There he gives the picture of the Christian torn, baffled, discouraged, and powerless to deliver himself. Many a young Christian in this state gives up, assuming that there is no victory and thus enters a miserable life of up and down experience—usually more down than up.

Why does he not enter into a life of victory instead? Because he seeks for it in himself and in what he can do. He forgets that he faced just as great an impossibility when he was brought under conviction for his sins. Then he came to an end of himself and simply trusted Christ for forgiveness of his sins. Now he finds himself in bondage to sin from slavery to which his whole being cries out for deliverance. He strives unavailingly against sin, prays for release from it, and makes every effort in his own strength to get victory. The more he strives, the more desperate he becomes. Until he lets go and lets God set him free, despair will be his. Christ is the only Saviour from sin as He is from sins.

There is no overcoming of the flesh except in the death of Christ on the cross. Christ died, and you died with Him. Your sinful flesh was nailed to the cross when Christ was, and when He said, "It is finished" you died with Him. Christ then took you down into the grave and brought you forth a new creation. He died, you and all men died with Him, that He might impart to all a new life in rising from the grave. Now, by the power of the Holy Spirit, you can "mortify the deeds of the body." It was by the eternal Spirit that Christ offered Himself without spot to God, and it is by the eternal Spirit that you can have the victory in the conflict between the two natures. "Thanks be to God which giveth us the victory through our Lord Jesus Christ."

35

Obedience

"As obedient children, not fashioning yourselves according to the former lusts in your ignorance" (I Peter 1:14).

Your life is to be different after you become Christ's. Whereas you were a child of disobedience, you are now to be an obedient child. You are no longer to mold your character by the evil desires you used to cherish when you did not know any better. If Jesus Christ has taken you captive, you are to subject all your desires in obedience to rightful authority, not to let them run riot in your life. Your eyes have been enlightened and your conscience awakened. Now you know that the spirit of disobedience is the spirit of the world that is at enmity with God.

You must at all times obey God. He, your Creator and your Redeemer, has supreme and final authority over you. Heart obedience to the known will of God is essential to a Christian profession that is real. The definite and positive command is "Be ye doers of the word, and not hearers only" (James 1:22). Mere hearing hardens the heart; doing changes the character. Obedience to God is the way of blessedness.

Your obedience to God must be complete. Partial obedience is not obedience at all. There is no substitute for full and complete obedience. No sacrifice, no good works, no exalted feeling —nothing can take the place of simple, unquestioning obedience to what you know is the will of God. Not what you think but what God says is the standard by which you are to govern your actions. Not what you want but what God requires is the criterion for your daily walk with God. You can delight to do the will of God, but whether you please or not, you must obey Him.

You are to render obedience also to authority other than that of God. He has decreed that there should be authority in the family. You must recognize that God has placed authority in your parents, and you must obey them. The one exception is if obedience to their commands is opposed to your duty to God—something that does not often occur. Obedience to your parents is not to be merely outward; it includes an inward reverence as well as outward expression in acts. It is to be the outcome of respect and glad submission.

"Let every soul be subject unto the higher powers," says Paul in Romans 13:11. Existing authorities have been established by God. There is no authority except by God's permission. The abuse of power is not of God but the power itself is. It is your Christian duty to be obedient to all rightful authority in the state, in the school, in society in general, even if it should be corrupt. Wherever the governing power is lodged, it is an ordinance of God and is to be submitted to as such. If you resist the power, you set yourself against what God has established. "They that resist shall receive to themselves damnation," says Paul. It is not your responsibility if those in authority do wrong, but it is your responsibility to be obedient to authority so long as such obedience is not clearly disobedience to God.

God has placed authority in the church. You are, therefore, to be obedient to what it requires of you. However, such obedience is not to be blind obedience that gives no heed to the Word of God. You are to search the Scriptures so that you know what God requires. It is your privilege to express your views, but you are not justified in working at odds with what the majority in the church deem to be the right course to follow. So long as the church is in harmony with the teachings of God's Word, you are without excuse if you disobey.

36

Opportunity

"I must work the works of him that sent me, while it is day" (John 9:4).

It has been said that "God's best gifts are not things but opportunities." Opportunities are God-given but you must have vision to see them and readiness to seize them in the short time they are before you. Everywhere there is work that never has been done and needs that are not being met. "The reason a lot of people do not recognize an opportunity when they meet it is that it usually goes around wearing overalls and looking like hard work."

If you are in the right place, all sorts of opportunity open. Serving, even in humble tasks, puts you near the door of opportunity. Men whom God uses are men of industry. Gideon was on the threshing floor when God sought him out to become the deliverer of His people. Elisha was plowing with twelve yoke of oxen when Elijah passed by and cast upon him the mantle of service. Peter and Andrew were fishing when Jesus called them to be His disciples. Paul was zealously serving God, as he thought, when the Lord appeared to him and told him of the great work he was to do. Each of these grasped immediately his opportunity and gave up everything to follow God.

"Fools occasionally find opportunities, but wise men make them." To be ready for opportunity, you must have vision. Joseph's brothers called him a dreamer, but he saw God's opportunity when it came. In captivity he applied himself and kept God's favor in spite of strong temptation and unjust treatment. His heart preparation and his readiness gave him the big opportunity of becoming ruler of Egypt, second in power to Pharoah, and the saviour of his people. Daniel kept himself in line with the purposes of God and thus had outstanding opportunity to render valiant service to God and His people.

Don't wait for opportunity to hit you. Any chance you have to do good is the same as a command to undertake the task. Be busy doing something worthwhile until God sets before you greater opportunity. Busy men are always finding opportunities. Moses was busy with his flocks when God appeared to him at Horeb. David was busy keeping his father's flocks when God sent Samuel to anoint him king of Israel. Nehemiah was serving as cup-bearer to the king when God called him to lead His people back from captivity. The discipline of working at small tasks prepares you for doing greater tasks. The secret of success is faithfulness in doing whatever duty is at hand. Pass by no opportunity to do good in order to find a better one, for you will search in vain.

Many opportunities have been lost because they who could have grasped them were not ready when they came. Opportunity counts for success only if you are ready to take hold of it when it comes. You may find much you have lost but you will never find a lost opportunity.

But this does not mean that opportunity will never come again. Whenever you hear God's call and are obedient to it, you rise to higher levels, assume heavier burdens, achieve more worthwhile results, and reap more bountiful harvests for God. Every day God provides something for you to do, some service you can render for Him and His kingdom, some opportunity to be a blessing to those around you. "As we have therefore opportunity, let us do good unto all men, especially unto them who are of the household of faith" (Galatians 6:10).

When opportunity to be of service to God and to others is afforded you, be ready. Grasp it at once and do your best. Your saddest memories in time to come will be of your lost opportunities for serving God.

37

Possibilities

"With God all things are possible"
(Matthew 19:26).

That which is most impossible for us to deal with is self. In his fall man withdrew his nature from dependence upon God and made himself the center of his own life and activity. This world is under the curse of God because men and women are living for self. Into every phase and relationship of life self-love and selfishness enter. Self is the fly in the ointment at every spiritual feast; self obtrudes into the holiest of thoughts. As God searches us, we see this traitor to man and to God appear in such ugliness that we have to cry out in anguish, "My sinful self my only shame, my glory all the cross." Only God can deliver us from the incorrigible self which He sentenced to death on the cross of Christ.

Through the power of the Holy Spirit, the cursed self can be mortified in us. Bishop Moule makes this prayer: "Spirit of God, infill, possess my entire being, deeper and deeper still. In the depth of my nature, when I am least thinking about it, go on day by day as the antiseptic of my flesh and self-life. Antagonize it, work against it, keep it out of sight, keep it at the place of death with Christ." He then says that this is one of several divine possibilities we can know in this life. With God anything is possible, however impossible it seems to be to us.

It is possible for those who are willing to trust God for keeping and victory, to rely upon His promises and find their truth verified. God does what He says He will do, so He fulfils every promise He makes, if you but meet the conditions. You should not ignore or throw aside God's promises. He gives them to you for use.

It is possible to cast all your care upon Him and to enjoy deep peace in doing it. No problem is too great for God to handle. Much we do not know but one thing we do know: we cannot drift beyond the love and care of God. You can rest the weight of all your anxieties upon Him, for you are always in His care.

It is possible to have your thoughts and imaginations thoroughly purified through faith. You need not go around thinking uncharitable, unholy, impure, ungodly thoughts. You need not be enslaved to vile, ignoble, unrighteous imaginings. The Holy Spirit can so change your mind as to make its most secret workings acceptable in the sight of God.

It is possible to see the will of God in everything and to abide by it with singing instead of sighing. Everything God does is wise and good, so you can cheerfully receive from His hand anything He sends. Content with His will, you have His best, not His second best. Happy will you be when you have no will but God's.

It is possible to rejoice in the Lord always, whatever be your temporal lot, however trying to self your circumstances. Make God, not your temporal possessions, your earthly situation, your bodily comfort, your full stomach, your honor, your power, your reputation, your education, your position, or anything of time, your portion. Then you can rejoice in Him though you be stripped of all that self holds dear.

It is possible to become strong in the Lord and in the power of His might. Where you were once weakest, where once you failed to keep your strongest resolutions, where before you walked in a wrong way, you can, through Him who loved you and gave Himself for you, have a blessed sense of His presence to make self and sin powerless in your life.

These possibilities are the work of God. Because they are, the true experience of them will cause you to desire less and less of self and more and more of God.

38

Prayer Answered

"If we know that he hear us, whatsoever we ask, we know that we have the petitions that we desired of him" (I John 5:15).

Adoniram Judson said, "I never prayed sincerely and earnestly for anything, but it came. At some time—no matter at how distant a day—somehow, in some shape—probably the last I should have devised—it came. And yet I have always had so little faith! May God forgive me, and, while He condescends to use me as His instrument, wipe the sin of unbelief from my heart." When God inclines our heart to prayer, He inclines His ear to hear. We have reason to thank God that He does not answer all our prayers as we make them.

Much that perplexes us in our Christian experience is but answer to our prayers. We pray for patience and God answers by sending tribulation, because tribulation works patience. We pray for submission and God's answer is suffering, for we learn obedience by the things we suffer. We pray for unselfishness and God send us opportunities to give ourselves in sacrificing for others and in pouring out ourselves in serving them. We pray for humility and some failure of our plans or ambitions puts us low in the dust of self-abnegation.

We pray for strength and God sends us trials through the bearing of which we may become strong. We pray for love and God puts us with seemingly unlovely people and lets them say and do things which try the nerves and pain the heart that we may learn the longsuffering of love. We pray for victory and there comes a storm of temptation that we may develop faith, which is the victory that overcomes the world. We pray for a closer walk with God and He severs natural ties, allows our closest friends to misunderstand us, and calls upon us to walk apart from all human fellowship.

God answers prayer but His answers often surprise us. Sometimes we are surprised that He answers at all; sometimes we are surprised at the way in which He answers. Blessed are those who leave their prayers with God who knows when to give, and how to give, and what to give as well as what not to give. And blessed also are those who do not make the mistake of praying to God and then deciding things themselves.

Give God time to answer your prayers. George Muller prayed twenty years for the salvation of a certain man before he saw his prayer answered. One day is as a thousand years with the Lord and a thousand years as one day. He is not in a hurry. When the time is ripe, the answer will be forthcoming—in the way He sees fit to answer. Delays are not denials. Not always is it best for us that we receive the answer soon; we may need preparation of heart and soul for the answer before it is best that we receive it. Ever and always we can be sure that our loving Father will do what is for our highest good.

You can fail in getting answers to your prayers because you do not hold on long enough. Jesus taught "that men ought always to pray, and not to faint" (Luke 18:1). You must never grow weary of praying. Satanic opposition is aroused when you pray, and God may be ready to send the answer before it is possible for Him to get it to you. But "Satan trembles when he sees the weakest saint on his knees." If you but have faith to continue in persevering prayer, the answer will come at last, though it be delayed.

39

Problems

"We have not a high priest which cannot be touched with the feeling of our infirmities" (Hebrews 4:15).

Problems and conflicts will be yours in life, for they come to everyone. Met in the right way, these will work good to you. To meet them right, you must get rid of your petty self-feelings and bring yourself to face facts as they are and to profit from experience. If you are not in bondage to your feelings, you will tackle with courage the problems you meet and you will persevere patiently in solving them. But if your feelings are at war with one another, the conflict is a double one—inner and outer—and you may be defeated.

It is in the realm of the moral and spiritual that you need most to be free of self-feelings. There is a moral order exterior to you. Right is right because it is right. Your need is to maintain the standard expressed in these words: "Right is right even though nobody is right, and wrong is wrong when everybody is wrong." Never get the idea that right is something you develop in yourself, that the way you feel and think makes a thing good or bad. You cannot "get by with it" by refusing to face facts, by shirking responsibility, by dodging obligations, ignoring them, or denying that they exist. You may deceive others, but you cannot deceive your sense of right without suffering consequences damaging to your personality.

"God hath made man upright; but they have sought out many inventions" (Ecclesiastes 7:29). It is your nature to seek devices to satisfy your miserable self. Having lost God, being without faith in God, man is bound by his own self and his feelings. So long as he has faith only in himself and fears and suspects all other beings including his Creator, so long will he be at odds with himself and his own best interests, spiritual and moral. Your need is to put facts on the throne of your thought life and to abide by them, however you may feel. Let experience—your own and that of others—teach you how slavish it is to follow feelings.

Apart from God, there is no real meaning to life. These are the facts in which true values lie: God sent into the world His only Son who taught the way of God, lived the life of God among men, died on the cross for man, rose from the dead, and ascended into heaven where He now sits on the throne of God. He offers what you need, first, forgiveness and reconciliation, afterwards, all things needful to the life of God in the soul. Your relationship to God is not a matter of feeling, though entrance into it may have been attended by feeling. Your standing with God at any time—past, present, or future—is not dependent upon how you feel or do not feel. It is absolutely and wholly a matter of what Christ did for you when He died on the cross.

To God through Christ you can come for help in time of conflict and trouble. You cannot come too often or ask too much. Having accepted Christ as your Saviour, you can forget past sins and mistakes which God has already forgiven and forgotten. You need not let your feelings rule you or deceive you. Live by the Word of God which stands sure and true forever, however you may feel.

40

Renewal

"Be renewed in the spirit of your mind"
(Ephesians 4:23).

Everything earthly has to be renewed. No created thing is sufficient in itself; everything must receive from without the essentials for its sustenance. God the Creator of the universe and of the spirits that inhabit it, is also the Sustainer of the universe and all therein. His will is the energy of the universe. A creative energy that ceased to operate with creation would mean an exhausted universe and a dead creator.

The trees and all vegetation must drink of the rain that comes down from heaven and draw from the minerals God has placed deep in the soil. All animals, including the young lions that "roar after their prey, and seek their meat from God" wait upon Him "who giveth food to all flesh" (Psalm 104:21; 136:25). Man's life, in common with all other life, can be sustained only by renewal from God. It is necessary to take in food frequently to repair the waste of the body, and God who feeds the fowls of the air, provides food for us who are "much better than they" (Matthew 6:26).

Just as there is need for renewal of the body, so we must be renewed in soul by feeding upon the Word of God, by listening to the preached Word, or by bringing it sustenance through the use of other means of grace. Very soon, if the body is deprived of the right kind of food in the proper amount, health is impaired. If we neglect means of grace, we experience impairment of spiritual health. No one can live a normal Christian life without the diligent use of the Word of God and secret prayer. A Christian life without God is not one created by God; if God had begotten it, it could be sustained only by God.

Except as we are constantly renewed, we cannot withstand the ever recurring assaults of the perpetual enemy of our souls, the chastening of our heavenly Father, or the evil strivings within. However proper and right the outward appearance be, storms and tempests will surely bring downfall and destruction if there be not inner strength. "If we suffer the good to grow weaker, the evil will surely gather strength and struggle desperately for the mastery over us," with an outcome that will be disastrous.

"Be ye transformed by the renewing of your mind" says Paul in Romans 12:2. God has made provision for you but you must lay hold on the provision He has made and see to it that grace produces in you a saving change and then carries it on. As God works in you, you must cherish and cultivate new dispositions, new inclinations, new attitudes, new sympathies, new antipathies, an enlightened understanding, a tender conscience, right thoughts, a will bowed in submission to the will of God, and affections that are spiritual and heavenly. You are not to be what you were in your old sinful life. Old things are passed away, all things are become new; you are to live by new rules, to act from new principles, and to have new purposes.

The mind is the ruling part of your being, at least for this present life. Take heed to the spirit of your mind. Set a strict guard over all avenues of entrance to it. Keep it from being defiled by thought of sin and disturbed by trouble. Keep a conscience void of offense. Think upon the good and thereby keep out bad thoughts. Center the affections upon heavenly objects. Die to sin more and more and live to righteousness more and more and thus carry on the renewing until it be perfected in glory. Draw near to God in humble dependence and you shall find fulfilled the promise, "They that wait upon the Lord shall renew their strength."

41

Saving Others

"They that be wise shall shine as the brightness of the firmament; and they that turn many to righteousness, as the stars for ever and ever"

(Daniel 12:3).

In Tibet two men set out to go from one village to another in the bitter cold of winter. Before they had proceeded far on their way, both began to feel the effects of the intense cold. They came upon a man lying in the snow who had been overcome by the cold. One of the two travelers examined the helpless man. Finding that he was yet alive, he proposed to his companion that they carry the victim of the cold to safety. The other refused to help, saying that if they stopped to do this, they themselves would be overcome. When he found that his companion was determined to render assistance, this second man bid the first good-by and went forward alone. The compassionate man took his unfortunate fellowman on his back and proceeded on his way also. As he made his way along the difficult path, bearing his heavy burden, the effort brought warmth to his body. He had nearly reached the village which was the destination for which the two had set out, when he came upon the body of a man lying dead in the snow. Upon examination, the good Samaritan found that it was the body of him who had refused to help carry the man the two had found.

One man through helping another saved his own life; another man unwilling to render assistance to a fellowman in deep need lost his own life. Glorious will be the reward of those who, in time of trouble and distress, are instrumental in helping others to find the way of righteousness. The more good the godly do in this world, especially to the souls of men, the greater will their reward be in the world to come. Those who forget their own interests and seek not to save their own lives but turn sinners from the error of their ways, helping to save their souls from eternal death, will share in the glory of those they have been the means of bringing to heaven. Children of God who by the mercy of God are faithful and successful in saving others shall shine very brightly in the next world—shall shine even as stars, with a light derived from Christ, the sun of righteousness.

Many through the centuries have been losers for Christ, even of life itself, but never was there, nor will there ever be, a loser in the end. There is a sure reward to those who are Christ's, who pour out their lives in unselfish devotion to Him and in compassionate love for the souls of men who are lost.

To be an instrument in saving a soul from eternal death is a joyous reward in itself. It means turning one from error; it means reclaiming one from the evil into which he has fallen; it means bringing him into the joy of the Lord; it means that he is turned from the power of Satan; it means that he receives forgiveness of sins and that he has an inheritance among them that are sanctified by faith in Christ Jesus. The saving of a soul includes the salvation of the whole man—the salvation of the spirit from hell, the raising of the body from the grave, and the saving of spirit and body from eternal death.

Why should you not be more concerned for the salvation of souls? Why should you not be more interested in the eternal happiness of the lost? By working for this, you can help prevent much evil and the spreading and multiplying of sin in the world, you bring glory and honor to your Lord, and you gain glorious reward for yourself. You can do now what will result in your shining as the stars forever and ever.

42

Security

"God is our refuge and strength, a very present help in trouble" (Psalm 46:1).

Danger, trouble, and weakness are the lot of man. We are always in danger. Some dangers we see; many are unseen. Daily, physical forces threaten the well-being of the body; we have no knowledge of many untoward conditions that could wreck our health and bring us down to the grave. The destructive forces of nature are unfriendly to us; some of them would snuff out our life in a second. Powers of evil are constantly working against the welfare of soul and spirit. Never are we safe from influences that could overthrow our reason. We spend our lives in the midst of dangers and trouble. Job could say, "Man is born to trouble, as the sparks fly upwards." So weak are we that we cannot cope effectively with untoward conditions we meet. Humanly speaking, we have no security.

But in God there is complete security. He is our refuge. He is a tower of strength into which we can run and be entirely safe. Whatever the danger, however terrible the trouble, we may flee to Him and He will protect and shield us. In the midst of dangers from without and from dangers within, He has promised to preserve and deliver us, and what He has promised He will do without fail.

God is our strength. We may not know how weak we are, but we do know that we are weak. It is by means of our conscious weakness that we become perfected in power as we, in faith, appropriate His strength. The strong person naturally glories in his physical strength, the one who thinks he is pure tends to glory in his moral strength, the religious person is inclined to glory in his supposed holiness. But the child of God says, "My strength is as the strength of omnipotence, because God is the strength of my life."

God is a help in time of trouble, a help always at hand, a help abundantly able for any and every situation, a help proved over and over again by countless men and women through the centuries of time. All around your helplessness, insufficiency, insecurity, and deep need flows the illimitable sufficiency of your all-powerful, ever-present, ever-living, ever-loving God. Human help, human sufficiency, human strength, is to no avail. As does each human being, you live in a little world of your own which no other human being can enter to bring you aid when you stand most in need of it. Like Job you will have experiences of trouble and danger which your best friends, with their desire to help you, will be entirely unable to cope with to your benefit. Because they are human, friends cannot be relied on; their hearts, the same as your own, are deceitful, and desperately wicked. God is not like man, untrue. Human strength, your own included, is only weakness at best; it is not possible for man to protect, preserve, or keep man. But, though all else give way, you have nothing to fear when God is your refuge and strength.

So you can say, "Come weal, come woe, come loss, come gain, come ease, come pain, come sorrow, come joy, come victory, come defeat, come danger, come trouble, I will trust Thee, O God, for thou art a very present help when all other helpers flee."

43

Selfishness

"Israel is an empty vine, he bringeth forth fruit unto himself" (Hosea 10:1).

Emptiness is the outcome of bringing forth fruit to self. God gives us talents and abilities to use for Him and for the good of our fellows. When we do not employ them for the use intended, turning the fruit they produce to our own advantage, we can expect nothing but to be emptied of them. It is a law of life that anything atrophies when not exercised in carrying out the purpose for which it was intended. So when a human being turns in upon himself those powers God gave Him to use for His glory and for helping others, he loses those powers. We cannot live selfishly and live full, complete lives.

Selfishness is sin. It is a sin against God, for it puts self instead of God on the throne of the heart. It usurps the place God should have in the life and gives it to self instead. Milton says of Satan that selfishness made him desirous of reigning in hell rather than of serving in heaven. The satisfaction of the creature, not doing the will of the Creator, is the aim and purpose of one who is guilty of the sin of selfishness. Once this sin takes possession of the heart, its victim stops at nothing that offers possibility of achieving his aim. Selfishness causes one who yields to it to worship self instead of God. Thus it sins against God in taking from Him the glory that is rightfully His.

It sins against God also in that it deprives Him of the fruit He has every right to expect from the life He created. To the maker of a thing belongs the increase that comes from what he makes. God made us, so we owe to Him the obligation to produce fruit unto Him. Bringing forth fruit to self is, therefore, stealing from God our Maker. If God has redeemed you through Christ, He has right to the fruit also of His creation. Thus selfishness becomes a greater sin when practiced by one who names the name of Christ.

Selfishness is a sin against our fellows. The selfish person seeks his own, not another's advantage. In so doing he deprives others of benefit belonging to them. The selfish person loves only himself, not his fellows, and, in centering affection on himself, he becomes guilty of taking from others the sympathy and the understanding due them. A selfish person cannot obey the commandment, "Thou shalt love thy neighbor as thyself." Even in praying he sins against others. "Lord, bless me and my wife, my son John and his wife, we four and no more," is not the type of prayer that reaches the throne. No selfish person can truly pray the Lord's Prayer, for it expresses not a single selfish plea. Not once does it say "me" or "my"; all the way through it is "Our" and "us."

Selfishness is a sin against one's self. He who lives only for self lives in vain. "He who lives only to benefit himself confers on the world a benefit when he dies." The victim of selfishness suffers more from his own selfishness than does the one from whom his selfishness prompts him to withhold benefit. Probably nothing hurts the spiritual life as much as selfishness. It is destructive of high attainment and it harms the person immeasurably. It cramps life, shatters lofty ideals, and blots out all that is elevated and noble. The essence of true nobility is lack of consideration of self, so as soon as the thought of self comes in, the beauty of a noble deed goes out. Selfishness brings neither satisfaction nor happiness to him who is bound by it.

Well may any of us make ours this prayer of a fellow mortal: "Deliver me, O Lord, from the evil man, myself."

44

Sickness

"This sickness is not unto death, but for the glory of God, that the Son of God might be glorified thereby" (John 11:4).

A devout native Christian visiting Adoniram Judson once when he was very sick, said, "Some sickness is of the devil, some sickness is for our discipline, some sickness is for the glory of God."

The devil afflicts us at times. By the permissive will of God, Satan can bring upon us many untoward things as he did in the case of Job. He is an adversary to God, to men, and to all good. Against Job, whom God commended for uprightness, godly fear, and hatred of evil, Satan not only cast base accusations but also brought upon him the sorest of afflictions, including terrible bodily suffering. But Satan is limited; he has not power to afflict God's children except as it is given him by God who allows to come into the life of none of His own anything he is not able to bear.

Sickness is a most valuable means of discipline—if we take the right attitude toward it. We can take any one of three basic attitudes. We may resent sickness, rail against it, chafe under it, blame ourselves or others, blame circumstances, blame God, and let it poison our whole being with bitterness. Or we can be unconcerned about it, take is as a matter of course, gather our own resources for coping with it, and stimulate our power of will to say, "All right, I can take it." Or we can welcome it as coming from God for our good. Our Lord teaches that we are neither to rebel against suffering of any kind nor simply to endure it but rather to accept it with gratitude. He encourages us to receive with thanksgiving, as submissive and trusting children, whatever God permits to come into our lives.

When we assume this last attitude, sickness, as any other seemingly untoward experience, proves to be a blessing in disguise. What is uncomfortable or painful to the body can be profitable to the soul. Anything that reminds us of the transitoriness of the temporal, anything that puts us in mind of our mortality, has a sobering effect upon us, bringing us to a proper sense of our duty and our destiny. Anything that brings home to us our helplessness is of worth to us, for, until we realize that we are helpless, Christ can do little toward living His life in us.

Some sickness is for the glory of God. It provides an opportunity for the manifestation of His power. It gives God opportunity to show favor to His child, whatever the manner in which He chooses to handle the case. The sweetest mercies are those coming out of trouble. God can show His favor and His glory by raising up the sick and restoring to health. But we must not put God to a test in a time of sickness by requiring Him to work a miraculous deliverance. This would be presumption. God's love and care and presence are real and are not to be measured by the nature of outward conditions, either favorable or unfavorable to human thought. We are to trust Him and yield ourselves to Him, then let Him work as He will for His own glory.

All that comes into our lives is for the glory of God. Our sickness, our loss, our disappointment, can bring glory to Him. If God be glorified, we, His obedient and trusting children, will be satisfied with whatever He does. In His goodness, love, and power He will ever take care of us and suffer no evil to befall our souls.

45

Sin

"Whosoever committeth sin is the servant of sin" (John 8:34).

These are hard uncompromising words that express a stern truth. Sin is not something to be held in light regard, something to be toyed with, something we can play with as we do with a ball that we pick up and lay down at will. Sin is dangerous. Many have there been who thought of it so lightly that they invited it into their lives instead of keeping away from it as far as possible. Sin is so powerful that those who thus give it entrance suffer bitter consequences. When we dally with sin, we are not the master of sin; we cannot escape from its clutches when we will. It reaches out, so to speak, and binds us inexorably.

You know for yourself that, in spite of all your strong efforts to banish sin from your life, it remains as an ugly fact. Likely, all of us have had the experience of being shocked by a sinful act we have done. It was as if we had not done the act at all. When you do such a thing, you probably ask in thought at least, "Is it possible that I did that?" It seemed as if something powerful had grasped you and compelled you to do what you really did not want to do. This brings to mind the words of God to Cain after he had murdered his brother Abel; "If thou doest not well, sin lieth at the door" (Genesis 4:7). Sin crouches at the door of our being like a powerful, ravenous beast that is waiting to overpower and destroy us as soon as we give it the slightest chance. Safety lies in being constantly on guard lest we give it the least occasion to enter. Once it is in, there is little we can do.

Paul, a man of exceptionally good character, faultless in his obedience to the law, was aware that he had in him "all manner of concupiscence" or evil desire. He knew that in his flesh dwelt no good thing and that he could not give the least place to evil, except at his peril. Since Adam fell into sin, all men have a diseased longing which expresses itself strongly toward what is forbidden of God and destructive of the soul. This sinful longing of our old nature leads us to believe in the fair promises of sin but it will take us to the portals of death if we follow its leadings.

The terrible truth is that one who sins is the servant of sin. It has power over him that he cannot break, strive as he may. Sin has power in the corrupt nature of every one of us. So long as we live in the flesh, we shall never see it entirely conquered in our lives. "There is enough tinder in the heart of the best of men to light a fire that shall burn to the lowest hell, unless God shall quench the sparks as they fall," says Spurgeon. However holy we may become, we shall always need to be kept back from the foulest sins. Of ourselves, we can expect nothing but to be overcome and destroyed.

But sin, with all its power, with our utter and complete powerlessness to contend successfully against it, has its master. Its power is not so great as that of Him who came forth from God to conquer sin and death. Never need we despair, however much we may be humbled by sin. We are exceedingly weak, but we have a powerful Saviour. He came to save us not only from our sins but also from the power of sin. With Paul, we have to exclaim, "Wretched am I!" and, in utter despondency, ask "Who can save me from this terrible lower nature that ever draws me toward the jaws of death?" But with Paul we can also say, "Thank God, deliverance is mine; Jesus Christ has brought freedom from sin and death."

"If the Son therefore shall make you free, ye shall be free indeed" (John 8:36). There is no other hope; nothing more is needed.

46

Suspicion

"Trust ye not in a friend, put not confidence in a guide" (Micah 7:5).

"A man prone to suspect evil is mostly looking in his neighbor for what he sees in himself." But is not suspicion sometimes justified? Don't unsuspecting people become the victims of those who have no regard for the rights of others? Certainly these questions must be answered with a "yes." What, then, should you do? When should you suspect? When should you not suspect?

To answer these last questions, it may be well to distinguish between suspicion and caution. Suspicion is a vague belief or fear concerning what may happen, based on no substantial reasons. Caution is the examination of facts and of probable effects to safeguard against danger or misfortune. It is not necessarily wrong to suspect; outcomes may prove that your suspicions were well-founded. It is normal to suspect at times. But when you suspect, get the facts, question, ascertain the truth, get the doubt out into the light. This is caution. Clinging to uncharitable thoughts, keeping on the lookout for opportunities to suspect, and refusing to be reasonable is suspicion.

In time the bitterness of suspicion will sear your being. You yourself create the enemies you dread or the situation you fear. "Suspicion is no less an enemy to virtue than to happiness; he that is already corrupt is naturally suspicious; and he that becomes suspicious will quickly be corrupt," observes Samuel Johnson.

How can you stop being suspicious? First, you must learn to recognize the evidences of suspicion. When you realize that you are beginning to become suspicious, face the situation. Ask yourself if you are allowing imagined ideas to color your judgment, if you are harming a fellow-man by your over-active imagination. Suspicion is far more likely to be wrong than right, and it is more frequently unjust than just.

Then ascertain why you read into the actions of another, or others, what is not there. Is it due to lack in yourself, as the outcome of your past mistakes, or is it caused by your lack of faith in the integrity of those you suspect? Suspecting others is often an outcome of unconsciously condemning yourself. You may be helped by the wisdom in Disraeli's observation: "It is much easier to be critical than to be correct."

You need to learn to evaluate suspicions. The ability to suspect the right things at the right time is an asset, but this ability must be trained and disciplined. Ability to detect what is in other people's minds can often be used in profitable ways. If you can read meaning into the actions of others you will be able to sense their needs, likes, and dislikes. Thus you will be in position to render service to them. If you are expert in jumping to conclusions, don't squelch the ability. Make it a practice to form several possible conclusions and to weigh each against the other until you ascertain which one is correct.

Don't live in everlasting suspicion of evil such as haunts the guilty mind. But remember that well-founded suspicion, or caution, avoids many evils that credulity or misplaced trust brings upon one. Trust should always be conditioned by charity but founded on reason. What you need to steer clear of is unguarded trust in any human being, including yourself.

47

Temptation

"Every man is tempted, when he is drawn away of his own lust, and enticed" (James 1:14).

Two men, both slaves to strong drink, were saved and began to live for Christ. Both gave up their habit of indulging in alcoholic liquor. One was always a bit fearful lest the craving for it might overpower him. He did all he could to keep away from it. Rather than expose himself to the danger of falling, he would walk around the block to avoid passing the door of a tavern. He kept out of the company of his old companions. He never took another drink. The second man boasted of his strength to withstand the temptation to drink. In the confidence that he could resist this temptation, he entered the tavern where his former companions were assembled. They took hold of him, dragged him up to the bar, and placed under his nostrils a glass of strong drink. The fumes from the liquor aroused such a craving for its effects that he drank it and fell back into his old ways.

The devil is called the tempter, and he may tempt you in many ways. However, neither the devil nor any other person or thing is to be blamed so as to leave you without excuse. There is in everyone evil which can be set on fire by temptation from without. "Can a man take fire in his bosom, and his clothes not be burned?" (Proverbs 6:27). The fire of lust in one kindles the fire of hell. The devil is always on hand to use our lusts to entice us into sin and to entangle us in a web of evil that will end in our eternal destruction.

No one is free from the possibility of being drawn into temptation by the evil within him. You never become so strong that it is impossible that you might be drawn away by evil desire and enticed into sin. Jesus said to Peter who thought himself strong, "Watch and pray, that ye enter not into temptation: the spirit indeed is willing, but the flesh is weak" (Matthew 26:41). Only the grace of God can keep you. The words of John Wesley, voiced when he saw a poor broken fellowman lying in the gutter, can well be your words too: "There but for the grace of God lies John Wesley."

What can you do to help make God's grace operative by way of keeping you from entering into temptation? For one thing, do as the first man of the illustration did: stay as far away from the place of temptation as you can. Avoid the way of evil, turn from everything that savors of evil, separate yourself from those who are inclined to put temptation before you. Second, keep busy at good. You cannot do two things at the same time. Occupied with good, being where good is done, in the company of those who are engaged in doing good, you definitely reduce, if you do not eliminate entirely, the possibility of being tempted. And, if you are tempted—for you never get into any situation where temptation cannot come—the enticement to enter into evil is far less strong or entirely absent.

Third, practice the presence of God. He is always near and the promise is that, if you draw nigh to Him, He will draw nigh to you. Neither evil nor the devil can stand in the presence of God. He is a sure refuge in every time of temptation. Pray. Ask God to deliver you from temptation, to keep you from yielding to temptation, to preserve you from the inducements of the devil. God hears and answers prayer. Trust in the work of Christ. He was tempted in all points like as you are but never entered into sin. Therefore, He is able to succor you when you are tempted. There is for you as there was for your Lord a way of escape from temptation without yielding to it.

48

Things to Come

"The Revelation of Jesus Christ, which God gave unto him, to show unto his servants things which must shortly come to pass" (Revelation 1:1).

God exists and carries out His purposes through the ages. We can believe in Him or not; whether we do or do not believe has no effect either on the fact of His existing or of His carrying out His plans. In the sight of God there are two classes of men—those who believe on Jesus Christ in whom God has revealed Himself and those who do not believe, rejecting the revelation He has made. "Things which must shortly come to pass" relate to God's dealings with these two classes of men.

For those who believe there is going to be a revelation of the glory of Christ in and with the redeemed. Christ is the life of the believer. Some day He is coming back to receive believers unto Himself. Christ is a glorious Lord—far more glorious than we know. In the plan of God, those whom Christ has redeemed are to share with Him the glory that is His with the Father. When Christ appears, these vile, sinful bodies of ours are going to be transformed so as to be like Christ's glorious body. How great and wonderful this transformation is going to be is beyond our power to imagine at present. The very best Christian is now far from being what he is going to be when Christ is revealed. "When he shall appear, we shall be like him; for we shall see him as he is" (I John 3:2).

Also, for those who believe there is going to be a restoration of God's rule on earth. Christ who ascended to heaven will return to earth and set up His kingdom and, with the redeemed, rule righteously and justly. Of this God has told us through the prophets of ages past. There are various views of how and when this restoration is to take place. No man can give all the answers to the questions that are raised. God has not seen fit to speak clearly of the details concerning "things which must shortly come to pass." But, of one fact we can be most certain: God is going to carry out His divine purpose and, if we believe on Him, we shall be sharers in everything that has to do with the fulfilment of that glorious purpose. Ultimately, He is going to make all things new in a new heaven and a new earth. Then shall those who have been made righteous through faith in Christ come into full and eternal possession of the marvelous things that God has prepared for them.

Things to come means for unbelievers a revelation also, but a revelation of righteous retribution. In flaming fire, God will take vengeance on those who reject the gospel of the Lord Jesus Christ. These shall receive the punishment of eternal destruction, because they refused to accept the truth but chose unrighteousness. They will be exiled eternally from the glorious presence of the wonderful God. He is no respecter of persons, so those who would not have His Son rule over them shall suffer His righteous indignation and wrath, whatever their profession and standing among men. Ultimately, they shall be cast into the lake of fire.

This life is the time to prepare for things to come. Now is the day of salvation, now unbelieving man may repent of his evil ways, become a believer, and thereby a child of God possessed of the blessed hope. The gracious invitation is extended to all. Today, "the Spirit and the bride say, Come. And let him that heareth say, Come. And let him that is athirst come. And whosoever will, let him take the water of life freely" (Revelation 22:17).

49

Today

"Sufficient unto the day is the evil thereof"
(Matthew 6:34).

Live today. To do so, you will have to eliminate what remains of the past. Let the death of each day be the death of the burdens of that day. Put no trust in tomorrow; it is vain to place your hopes in a morrow that will never come. Today is the day the Lord made for you; when tomorrow comes, it will be today. Rejoice in it, be glad in it. Live today—fully, richly, completely.

More and more the evidence points to the fact that for you there may be no tomorrow. This was always true of individuals, but now it is being brought home to us that, as a race, we may at any moment be destroyed.

You are not living in the world your parents and their parents knew. You cannot live today as people lived in 1875 or even in 1935. In recent years the world has changed suddenly and radically. Now as you look upon the nuclear forces which man has unleashed, you may wonder if the end of civilization may not be at hand. If such forces should be turned to destructive purposes, men will be helpless before them. And who knows whether these forces will one day be used as weapons of war, or whether, in the mercy of God, they will always be turned to peaceful purposes?

The future threatens you, the past offers you no help. What can you build on today? The mere asking of the question may trouble you. There are no means by which you can be given understanding of the changes that are occurring in the world in which you live and how to cope with them. Humanly speaking, you have right to be afraid. Do you want to exercise that right? Do you want to go tremblingly on your way to destruction or at least the thought of destruction? It is easy to do this, but you can resist the tendency; you need not follow sheep-like the dark road. You can stop and look up and lift up your eyes to the light that shines for you.

For the light does shine, however dense the darkness, no matter what the evil men devise. You have Christ's word: "All power is given unto me in heaven and in earth" (Matthew 28:18). God who rules the stars in their courses controls the affairs of men and nations, over-ruling their actions to the carrying out of His own purposes. If you are His child through the redemption that is in Christ, you are entirely within His power and care. "Even the very hairs of your head are all numbered" (Luke 12:7). With the complete confidence you may have in Him, you can live with rejoicing, knowing that He gives you this present time in which to serve Him.

You cannot do anything about the forces of destruction that are at work in the world. But you can maintain toward these forces the right attitude; you need not live in slavish fear of what they might do to you and to the world in which you live. You can give yourself to the present and, in doing this, you can live vctoriously. For you have God's own assurance: "As thy days, so shall thy strength be" (Deuteronomy 33:25). All things are in His hands who has promised to supply your needs for each day that He gives you.

Today is yours, and today alone. Yesterday is past. God alone knows whether or not you will be on this earth tomorrow. But today you are favored with the gift of life. Today is the possession God has given you, to use for His glory with all the strength that is in you. Angels and fellow-spirits bid you gird up your soul and live—today—joyfully, fully, in the confidence that you are Christ's, and in Him, all things are yours (I Corinthians 3:21–23).

50

Trial

"The trial of your faith, being . . . precious" (I Peter 1:7).

Trial is the lot of the Christian. The world is opposed to God and to those who are God's, so it offers children of God no help in living for Him. In the twelfth verse of the fourth chapter of this epistle, Peter tells us not to think it strange that fiery trial come to test us, as though some surprising thing had befallen us. God's people are a tried people. The father of faith, Abraham, was a tried man, and all men of faith since his day have been tried men.

The troubles and the afflictions of Christians have for their purpose the trial of faith. God's design in permitting affliction to come is to test us, not to harm us; to help us, not to ruin us. A trial is a test made upon one, by some affliction or trouble, to prove the genuineness and the strength of his faith. This trial is made upon faith mostly, instead of some other grace, because faith is the foundation of all in relation to God. Faith is both the source and the mainstay of the life of God in the soul. Christ prayed for Peter that his faith fail not when he was tried. If faith fails not, all else will stand firm. The faith of the child of God is tried in order that he may have the blessing of stronger faith, others the benefit of his faith, and God the glory from his faith.

What should be your attitude toward trial? The proper attitude is one of rejoicing. You ought not merely to be patient but to rejoice in sufferings for Christ, for these are evidences of divine favor. A man said of a fellow Christian who was being sorely tried: "God must love him a lot, for He gives him much suffering." Suffering and trial prepare you for glory. The trial of your faith is precious because, by it, faith is established and made stronger and deeper. Through trial, God and the actualities of the unseen world become more real.

Faith untried may be genuine faith, but it is sure to be little faith. It will likely remain small so long as it is not tried. After Abraham was tried, he became a man "strong in faith, giving glory to God" (Romans 4:20). Faith thrives best when things are against it. Trials are its trainers, and afflictions are its source of strength. When you are tried, your faith grows. Tried faith brings experience; you would never know how weak you are had you not met trial; you would never have learned to appropriate God's strength if you had not been supported by Him in time of affliction. Faith increases in depth and strength the more it is exercised through trial.

Does this discourage you? Do you think that a young person cannot be strong since he has not had much experience? Be assured of this: if you walk with God, you will have trials enough without wishing for them and seeking them. In due season, God in love and wisdom will see that the full portion is measured out to you. Meanwhile, though you cannot claim the benefits of much experience, you can thank God for what grace you have. You can praise Him for whatever degree of confident faith in Him you have attained by His grace. If you live according to this rule, you shall have more and more blessing from God, and your faith will grow stronger and stronger.

51

Understanding the Bible

"Thy word is a lamp unto my feet, and a light unto my path" (Psalm 119:105).

The most learned scientist in the world does not know what electricity is, but no person is so ignorant that he cannot use electricity and enjoy its benefits. God has set before men a way of life and has given men a written Word telling them of this way. Isaiah says that God's way of holiness can be followed unerringly by wayfaring men though they be fools. God gives men the things they need, and He gives them the knowledge necessary to use those things. The truth He has revealed to us is infinitely more important to us for our temporal and our eternal welfare than would be understanding of the mysteries He in wisdom sees fit to conceal from us.

Ask the man who has devoted his life to the study of the Bible if he can understand everything in it, and he will answer "No." Ask the most consecrated Christian you know if he understands the Bible, and he, too, will answer "No." But his face will glow with a light not seen on land or sea as he goes on to say, "I love the Bible even if I don't understand everything in it. I understand some things I once did not understand. The longer I live, the more I expect to understand things that are not clear to me now. And some day I will understand everything."

For us here and now, on this little shoal of time, there is something more important than understanding everything in the Bible. It is this: If we do the things we do understand, we shall be kept so busy that we will not have time to worry about the things we do not understand. God gives us all the light we need for the life He would have us live, for the duties He would have us perform. If we walk in the light He gives, we will have light for advancing on the way. One walking in the night, bearing a light to guide his steps, need not see what is far in front of him. As he moves along, the light advances also, showing him step by step the way he is to go, revealing to him the pitfalls he must avoid and the dangers he must escape. Likewise, as we walk in the way of the Lord, light shines on our path as we need it. "Then shall we know, if we follow on to know," says Hosea.

There is light sufficient for each of us as we travel the trackless wastes of this vast, unfriendly, dark world. God lets none without witness to Himself. He deprives no one of the amount of light he needs. "I am the light of the world," said Jesus, "he that followeth me shall not walk in darkness, but shall have the light of life" (John 8:12). Not a single one of us is without light; every one of us understands enough of the Bible to be kept busy in doing the will of God. After all, God does not require that we be "understanders" but that we be first, believers, then doers of the Word. And it is doers who are blessed in their deeds. Far better is it to understand little and humbly obey than it is to know much without doing what we know we should do. God will ever see to it that we know His will if we but be willing and obedient in doing His will as far as we know it.

And after we have lived long years and gained much understanding of the Bible, we shall be obliged to admit that we have only begun to understand it.

52

The Walk of the Christian

"He that saith he abideth in him ought himself also so to walk, even as he walked" (I John 2:6).

Are you a Christian, or do you just say that you are a Christian? Has Christ saved you from your sins, or are you nothing more than a baptized, unregenerate sinner? Do you have the life of God in your soul, or are you only one who professes to belong to Christ? Do you live as Jesus lived, or do you live as men of the world live?

A young man attending medical school, the only Christian in the student body, had considerable difficulty in adjusting to the situation until he came to this realization: "I am different, and I will just have to be different." A Christian is essentially like other people in general appearance. But he is not at all like other people in his nature. He has a new nature, a life that comes from God—the life that Jesus lived—in his soul. And this life is manifest in what he does. Being in union with God through Christ, he must live as Jesus lived.

What are some of the ways in which you will walk if you live as Jesus lived? First, you will walk in complete submission to God. You will say as Jesus did, "I must be about my Father's business" (Luke 2:49); "My meat is to do the will of him that sent me" (John 4:34); "I do always those things that please him" (John 8:29); "Not my will, but thine, be done" (Luke 22:42). Not only will you say such words, but you will count no cost too great, not even life itself too dear, to come in the way of absolute obedience to all the known will of your heavenly Father.

If you walk as Jesus walked, you will walk in love to all people.

He did not just say that He loved, but He demonstrated His love in living for and in dying for those He loved. His love went out to the unlovely as well as to the lovely, to those in whom there was nothing, naturally speaking, to call forth love. He loved when those He loved went astray, when they were contrary, when they spurned His love, when they misrepresented Him and when they completely rejected Him. Nothing—absolutely nothing—could quench His love and its expression in deed, even unto dying for those He loves.

If you walk as Jesus walked, you will live righteously. Righteousness is much more than a matter of outward conduct; it is holiness in expression; it is the fruit of a holy state or condition of heart; it is the expression in conduct and manner of living of the life of God in the soul.

If you walk as Jesus walked, you will live in complete abhorrence and utter intolerance of known sin. You are not, of course, a sinless being as was Jesus. Daily, as the catechism says, we sin in thought and word and deed. But the child of God is sensitive to sin and does not willingly give it a place in practice. If you are a child of God, it is true that you may fall into sin; the old nature will at times prevail in spite of your relationship with God. But you will not live in deliberate sin, for the new nature, being from God, cannot sin. "Whosoever abideth in him sinneth not: whosoever sinneth hath not seen him, neither known him" (I John 3:6).

53

Witnessing

"Ye shall be witnesses unto me" (Acts 1:8).

Dr. Pentecost tells of calling upon an outstanding business man to speak to him about Christ. He made the call in fear and trembling, with an air of apology. But the business man, deeply moved, said, "Don't ever hestitate to speak to any man about his soul. I've waited twenty years to have someone speak to me."

Do you associate daily with people who may be waiting for you to speak to them about the claims of Christ upon them? It is God's plan that those who come to know Him in Christ should tell others about their Saviour. Every Christian should be a witness to the saving power of his Lord. Yet there is perhaps no duty that Christians shirk more frequently. Into the heart of every person born of God, the Holy Spirit has come to dwell. The Spirit prompts Christians to bear witness to Christ. But over and over again Christians quench the Spirit and fail to act upon this prompting.

Why do Christians thus quench the Spirit? Why do they fail to witness for their Lord? Satan gains a victory when you allow excuses to keep you from telling people about Christ. It is Satan's definite purpose to prevent you from witnessing. He may cause you to be afraid to approach a person on the subject of his soul's welfare. He may make you believe you are not good enough, that you fall too far short of being the kind of a Christian that you ought to be. If Satan cannot stop you in such ways, he may cause you to believe that it is of no use, for people have heard the gospel, and if they wanted to accept Christ, they would have done so already. If Satan fails in this, he may say that the preacher, not you, should do the work of winning souls.

To be a witness, you will have to resist Satan and speak. But you must remember that there are right ways and wrong ways to witness. You cannot win a soul by going to the person with the attitude of condemning. That will very likely drive him away from Christ who came not to condemn but to save. Your work is to present Christ, not to condemn. Your witness will have effect only if your heart is filled with supreme love to God and deep love for souls. Never should you undertake to witness without prayerful dependence on God. Only God can change a human heart. Pray in advance, asking God to draw to Himself the soul in which you are interested. Ask God for love, wisdom, courage, and guidance. Pray while witnessing that the Spirit may speak to him with whom you are dealing.

Use your Bible. Let God speak to the soul through His Word. Your words may fail to make any impression, but God's Word has authority. You need not wait until you gain superior knowledge of the Bible. The thought that you must, may be another of Satan's numerous devices to keep you from witnessing. Many a soul has been won through the use of a single verse, especially John 3:16. It is well to have the person you are dealing with read for himself the Bible passages you use.

Tell him how you came to know the Lord. He cannot deny what you know has happened. That you found Christ is evidence that your hearer can find Him too. Be lovingly urgent, for a soul's eternal welfare is at stake. Let the Holy Spirit use you in leading the person to repent of his sins and to accept Christ as Saviour.

54

You

"Are not five sparrows sold for two farthings, and not one of them is forgotten before God? . . . Fear not therefore: ye are of more value than many sparrows" (Luke 12:6, 7).

Why are you here? Why were you born? Life is a road upon which you find yourself travelling. Behind you is a vast eternity of the past; ahead of you is another inevitable vast eternity. You did not ask for this life that is in between the two eternities, but you have it to live. What are you going to do with this little earthly span of time?

No thinking being can deny that a supreme Person created an orderly universe, with its immutable laws. Since this is true, then there must be for you, as for every human being, a true purpose in life. God would not bring into existence a universe for which He conceived a complete plan, then let man blunder along, a foreigner to His thought and care. "Life is a mission," says Mazzini. And he goes on to say further, "Every other definition of life is false, and leads all who accept it astray. Religion, science, philosophy, though still at variance upon many points, all agree in this, that every existence is an aim." God who forgets not the sparrows that are sold at the rate of five for two cents, will not forget you, because you are of far more value.

The world would not be what it is if you had not been born. You have added something to it that was not here before you came out of the eternity of the mysterious past. What you have added is from God and it is of immense value. If you do not use your life in the best way, if you do not seek diligently to develops its powers, you deprive God of an outlet He put you in the world to supply. No one can take your place; if you fail, the loss is irreparable.

No two blades of grass were ever alike, no two leaves on all the trees of all time were ever alike, no two snowflakes in all the snowstorms this world has ever seen were just the same. Faces, hands, voices, personalities all differ. Of the multiplied billions of people who have walked the earth, there have never been two who were alike. God made each person different from every other person, and each is important in His plan for all. You have a contribution to make to the carrying out of that plan. Don't belittle yourself. Don't think that what you are and what you do does not matter. You may be a "nobody" among the millions on earth, you are only a tiny drop in the vast ocean of humanity, but you are important to God.

Of course, you are only one, but you are one. God gave to you something He gave to no other person. The way you use what He gave you is important to Him. You may not be able to do what more gifted men and women can do, but what you can do, you ought to do for the glory of God. The greatest danger you face is that of doing nothing, because you cannot do what you deem to be the great things and will not do what you think are little things.